A PLACE TO SHINE:
EMERGING FROM THE
SHADOWS AT WORK

A PLACE TO SHINE:

Emerging from the Shadows at Work

DANIEL S. HANSON

Butterworth–Heinemann

Boston Oxford Melbourne Singapore Toronto Munich New Delhi Tokyo

Butterworth–Heinemann
℞ A member of the Reed Elsevier group
Copyright © 1996 by Daniel S. Hanson

∞ Recognizing the importance of preserving what has been written, Butterworth-Heinemann prints its books on acid-free paper whenever possible.

Library of Congress Cataloging-in-Publication Data

Hanson, Daniel S., 1945–
    A place to shine: emerging from the shadows at work/Daniel S. Hanson.
      p. cm.
    Includes bibliographical references and index.
    ISBN 0–7506–9738–5 (pbk.)
    1. Job satisfaction.   2. Interpersonal relations.
    3. Organizational behavior.   I. Title.
    HF5549.5.J63H28   1996
    650. 1´3—dc20   95–39382
                                                  CIP

British Library Cataloguing-in-Publication Data
A catalogue record for this book is available from the British Library.

The publisher offers discounts on bulk orders of this book.

For information, please write:

Manager of Special Sales
Butterworth–Heinemann
313 Washington Street
Newton, MA 02158–1626

10 9 8 7 6 5 4 3 2 1

Printed in the United States of America

To Joel,
who taught me to pay attention to the right things.

Table of Contents

Preface

A few years ago, I was told that a lump in my neck was cancer. Upon learning the diagnosis, I went through the usual pattern. I experienced all the crazy thoughts and feelings that the experts told me I would. Several questions raced through my mind all at once, questions like: Am I going to die? Why me? Is the prognosis as good as they say it is? Surely, the doctors are keeping something from me. Even if we stop the cancer now, will it come back? If so, where? When?

Strange as this may sound, cancer has had a positive influence on my life. It forced me to let go of my need to show the world that I could work harder than anyone else. It gave me permission to be silent, to revisit my childhood, to read my experiences in a new light and to reacquaint myself with insights from authors and wise mentors who have impressed me over the years. I took time out to reflect on who I had become and where I was spending my time and energy. In the middle of my battle with cancer I learned how to play again, to let go of some of life's control mechanisms long enough to truly enjoy nature, people, and the world around me that had helped shape who I had become. I learned to appreciate the whole of myself—not just the good parts. I learned to embrace the shadows of my past and to love myself for who I was becoming, with all my human frailties, and to love others with the same unconditional acceptance. I set aside my well-programmed life long enough to write this book.

All this reflecting awakened some dormant feelings deep within me. Some of my crazy feelings were unexpected. I remember thinking about death and how surprised I was that I didn't fear it more than I did. For me, death was easier to face than a life without meaning. Sadly, I reflected on the lack of meaning in my own life and in the lives of other people I knew.

Why am I telling you about my personal life? What difference does it make that I have battled cancer as so many others have?

I believe that it is important for each of us to share what we learn from living, especially those insights we gain when the forces of life itself take us on a journey to places where we are asked to confront ourselves and our view of the world around us, including the parts we do not understand or perhaps are not so proud of—the "shadows," as Carl Jung named them. In the middle of these journeys we often discover truths about ourselves and our world. In my own case, these discoveries shaped much of the thinking contained in this book.

Having lived through an almost fatal auto accident in my twenties, my midlife bout with cancer was the second time I had been forced to step back and reflect on my life. And I discovered valuable truths on both occasions. But this time I came to realize a simple truth that changed the direction of my life. It is a truth about life that I probably knew all along, but could never quite articulate. Let me try to explain it.

We search in this life for three things: a self to be, others to love and be loved by, and meaningful work to do. All three are related in a very spiritual way. In Western cultures we spend much if not most of our time at something called a "job." It is defined by organizations we work for and consumes the majority of our waking time. Experts tell us that we *are* our work, that our very self-esteem is based on the job we hold. But many of the jobs we hold do not leave room for discovering meaning in work, nor do they encourage us to share our work with others we love. As a result, the self, work, and others to love got disconnected. Parts of us got separated from the whole. We were encouraged to leave our hearts at home and to work only with our heads.

About this time in my reflecting I came upon a metaphor. It grew out of a little song I learned in the second grade. The song was called "This Little Light of Mine" and it was about shining. The "shining" metaphor took on energy as I shared it with people at work and the students in my classes. We talked about the need to shine in our work. We concluded that people shine in their work only when their work connects them to the special gifts that are part of who they are, and when they feel appreciated and confirmed in the presence of others who count in their lives.

As I reflected further, it occurred to me that not very many people I knew were shining in their work. The very systems we had created to work more efficiently and effectively had grown so big and complicated that they were casting shadows. People felt disconnected from their work and each other. They were walking around in the shadows of the organization, looking for meaning and purpose. Some had given up and fallen asleep in the shadows, working Monday through Friday in daily anticipation of the weekend. Others swore allegiance to the organizational imperative of growth and profits only to discover that parts of them had fallen asleep. In too many cases, their hearts had fallen asleep. At this point, I wondered what would happen to our organizations, and our society for that matter, if we helped each other to shine in our work.

There is one more lesson from my personal journey that I must share before I tell you more about this book and why I wrote it. As much as I learned from my encounter with cancer, I learned an even more valuable lesson from my son, Joel. Joel taught me how to capture the insights I had gained and the truths I had discovered while reflecting on my own life, and integrate them into my relationships to others and the world around me. While on a difficult journey of his own, he taught me how to pay attention to other people. Not in a trivial sense, but in the true sense of what the great philosopher Martin Buber called *making present*, a concept that goes beyond the popular notion of empathy and captures the all-absorbing encounter between two people who respect their uniqueness, yet share their common humanity—even to the extent that they realize the hurt they cause one another just by being human. It is a concept that is not easily captured in words, but those who have lost themselves for a time while caring for someone and connecting with them at a deeper level know what I am talking about.

Through my encounter with Joel, I came to realize that one of the biggest reasons people were not shining in their work was because a powerful ingredient was missing. The missing ingredient was the acceptance, affirmation, and confirmation of others.

At the end of this leg of my journey I concluded that the shadows at work were not all that different than those I had learned to embrace in my own life. Both had to do with being disconnected. I began to think that our organizations were battling a cancer of their own. Judging by the evidence, this would seem to be true. Almost every organization I knew was busy going through some kind of therapy, whether a quality movement, a reengineering process, or learning to be a learning organization. What's more, experts were telling us that something was wrong. They were saying that our organizations had lost touch with the customer. They told us that our systems had grown too big and costly to compete in a world of more nimble competitors. They offered models and formulas to help turn things around, to make us more competitive in the world.

Unfortunately, much of what we have been busy doing to fix our organizations have been surface cures. The cancer I am talking about has deeper roots. I am talking about a cancer that eats away at the very soul of our organizations: the relationships between people, their work, the people they work with, and purposes beyond the immediate. The cure for this cancer requires more than a quick-fix program. It calls for new relationships and a change of heart.

Who should read this book? You, the readers, are the best judge of that. But in the spirit of fairness, I will briefly describe its contents and structure so that you can make a more informed decision.

I know that every author says the same thing, but I must say it again anyway. This book is not for everyone. Indeed, if I had tried to make it so, I would have destroyed the message. This book is about shining at work, not because it will immediately improve the growth and profits of your organization or help you get more out of "your people." Rather, it is about shining at work for the pure sake of shining itself and the value of learning to connect with our work and each other—not just for ourselves and each other, but for our society and those who will work on this planet long after we are gone, including our children, grandchildren, and their grandchildren. Thus, if you are looking for a business book about turning the organization around to make it more profitable, you probably need to look for another book. At the same time, I truly believe that the organizations that will shine in the twenty-first century will do so because they are full of people who shine together in their work.

There are more differences between this book and others you might read about work and the changing organization. Perhaps the most important difference is the author. Not because my message is new or more profound than what is already out there. In truth, I doubt that there is anything new to be written about work and organizations, only resynthesis of knowledge that has been around for a long time. But as I often tell my audiences when asked the difficult question about the difference between my message and others like it: the difference is me. It is the stuff of life that I have experienced because I am me—especially the insights and truths I have gained from being wounded now and then. In the final analysis, what makes each of our messages unique is ourselves and our willingness to share what we believe from the heart. Perhaps that—along with personal knowledge, perspectives, and insights, based on experience and being wounded now and then—is all any author can offer.

Because every book bears the mark of its author, it often shows a bias based on the personal experiences and passions of the author. If there is a bias to this book it is toward building healthy relationships between people at work, relationships based on the belief that people shine when we accept them for who they are becoming and strive to confirm them, thus bringing out their true potential. It is the simple, yet difficult to practice, message that says we shine when we feel needed and appreciated. Perhaps I am sensitive to this message because I have been wounded in this spot and I personally know others who have as well. Nothing hurts more than feeling that one is not appreciated, that one's work does not count for much. You will probably see this message come through frequently. To me, it is one of the worst shadows in the workplace because it violates the sacred connections between people, their work, and the people they work with.

In many ways this book is really a simple metaphor called a place to shine. The metaphor is simple, but the task before us is not; yet simple metaphors can be powerful tools in the right hands. Sometimes they are more powerful than complicated models and theories. And we certainly have enough of those around these days. Furthermore, simple metaphors can act as a language to discuss complicated issues without trivializing them. If the metaphor is of value, it will draw the attention of other people who care about the same issues and grow from the energy of new insights and perspectives. It is my hope that a place to shine will grow to be a tool for healthy change.

The primary focus of this book is helping each other shine at work, but the message has meaning beyond the workplace. Everyone who has experienced the frustration of feeling trapped by her "job" or watched her efforts overshadowed by a complicated system will identify with the stories and reflections written here.

This book has three parts. The first part is about our need to shine—especially in our work. I point out that in order to shine in our work three things must be present: one, we must have work to do; two, there must be others to love and be loved by; and three, our work must be connected to a purpose that transcends the immediate. On a personal note, I share some faulty assumptions about shining that I have learned to question in my own life. In the final chapter of Part One, I offer a working definition of a place to shine. I close with three stories about people I have known who taught me what it means to shine at work.

In the second part of this book I explain why I think we are not shining at work. I identify the shadows cast by our organizations. I offer a simple model based on theories, structures, and scripts. I probe the theories that encouraged us to think about ourselves and our work in ways that gave the organization permission to use us as just another resource. I unveil the hierarchical power-based structures that put walls around us and caused us to become status-conscious, territorial, and alienated from each other. I hope to show how our everyday self-protecting scripts and rituals reinforced our distorted thinking, supported our hierarchical structures, and put out the light of the human spirit within, between, and around us. We were metaphorically going around killing each other's songs.

The third and final part of this book is an invitation to emerge from the shadows at work by embracing them, to take control of our work and our relationships by getting involved in the process of building places to shine. I suggest we put work in a new light and consider new, healthier theories, structures, and scripts. I offer a view of the process of transformation in the workplace that we are still going through and suggest ways to influence it in a healthy direction—toward a place to shine. In the final chapter I offer a model to help you on your own journey to a place to shine. I challenge all of us, myself included, to pay attention to the "right" things, to connect to our work and each other in new, even spiritual ways, and to learn how to shine where we stand and to confirm the "specialness" in each other—not just at work, but in our homes and in our communities as well—because the lines between work, home, and community are blurring. I assert that if we do not help each other shine, regardless of how work and organizations get redefined, we will have forfeited a rare opportunity for which we and those who follow us will pay dearly. Throughout the book I share stories about people who are building places to shine even in the midst of the shadows, in the hope that we might learn from their experiences.

At first, this book might seem like a message of doom and gloom. But if you read a bit further, I am convinced that you will begin to see a message of hope. According to the experts, for several years now we have been changing from an industrial era to an information age, or what some refer to as a digital age. Just the other day I read another article on how the access to information will transform our lives at work. The point is: transitions are times of opportunity. As old ways lose their effectiveness, we are given an opportunity to learn from our past mistakes and to build a better future. I believe that we have an opportunity to emerge from the shadows at work and shape the future beyond the information age, to introduce an age of truth and love that will inspire us to shine at work in ways not yet imagined, whether we express our work at home, in the community, or in the organization.

Regardless of the new forms, relationships will be the key to shining in our work. Because we truly shine only when we build spiritual relationships with our work, each other, and purposes beyond the immediate. I also know from embracing the shadows in my own life that healthy relationships are a powerful healer. Just being appreciated for who we are is a healing process in and of itself. Indeed, I have discovered that relationships can work miracles. Perhaps they can even turn places to work into places to shine.

Acknowledgments

I hesitated until the last deadline before entering these acknowledgments. I was so afraid that I would miss someone or fail to give credit where credit is due. But I decided to take that risk and ask those whom I might have forgotten or failed to properly recognize here, to forgive me and not to lose hope. I promise to express my gratitude in another, perhaps more personal, way.

First, I acknowledge my family: Sue, whose faith and love inspired me always; Troy, whose holistic thinking and willingness to read my early material kept me trying; Heidi, a poet in her own right, who made me feel like a special father; Harry, who believed in me; and Joel, who opened my senses to see, hear, and feel the "right" things.

Next in line are my friends: Rick Irvin, who has been my friend—it seems like forever; John Rebane, who not only shared my joy, but also hung in there with me when the going got rough and I needed the counsel of a friend; Bob Nechal, who has always been there for me, willing to speak from the spirit; David Hettinga, who truly convinced me that "a friend in need is a friend indeed"; Deb Schultz, my favorite "autotelic" person; Tom Bodin, who believed in me before I believed in myself; Kate Towle, an inspiration to whomever she touches; Rick Thoni, who was always there when I called; Pam Meier and Philip Stielstra, who kept me from compromising my work; Tobin Barrozo, whose wise counsel steered me along the right paths of thinking and opened new roads in my search for truth; my breakfast partner, Terry Donovan, who made me think and gave me more leads than I could ever follow up on; and Margaret Lulic, whose influence made this book a reality. A special acknowledgment to George Shapiro, who taught me the true meaning of unconditional acceptance and showed me with his own actions how to be present for others.

These acknowledgments would not be complete if I failed to mention the authors whose ideas I used to enhance my own. Their names appear in the list of references in the back.

Finally, I must acknowledge my partner in crime who helped put this work in order and get it into print. To Karen Speerstra, a professional, a partner, and a friend.

The basis for man's life with man is twofold, and it is one—the wish of every man to be confirmed as what he is, even as what he can become, by men; and the innate capacity of man to confirm in this way. That this capacity lies so immeasurably fallow constitutes the real weakness and questionableness of the human race: actual humanity exists only where this capacity unfolds.

. . . MARTIN BUBER

INTRODUCTION

As a boy I attended a one-room schoolhouse. There were four of us in my class, including me—all boys. Our second-grade teacher, Miss Madson, made us sing a little song almost every day. It went like this:

This little light of mine, I'm gonna let it shine,
This little light of mine, I'm gonna let it shine,
This little light of mine, I'm gonna let it shine,
Let it shine, all the time, let it shine!

As we grew older we balked at the requests to sing. After all, older boys didn't sing silly little songs about shining. But even as mature and worldly fourth graders we had to admit there was something magical about the song that made us feel appreciated and special. I stopped singing the song many years ago, I am sorry to say, except to share it now and then in a light moment with my own kids when they were little.

As I started to write this book about shining in our work I was reminded of the silly little song I learned as a child in a one-room schoolhouse. I remembered how good it felt to sing about shining. It made me feel shiny just to do it. I wondered why as adults most of us stop singing songs, except in church. Moreover, I wondered why we stop hearing the simple, yet profound messages that are often hidden in the lyrics of simple little songs, like the message that we all need to shine.

The passion that drives me to write this book is one that grew from a simple little song. It is the message that everyone, including you, needs to find a place to shine, a place where the light hits your special skill, creative flair, or personal perspective just right, a place where you are appreciated and confirmed as a special person by other people who care, a place where you are free to care for others, in turn, and even lose yourself in a purpose that transcends the immediate.

Unfortunately, many people are not finding a place to shine at work. Win/lose competitive views of the world, carrot/stick theories of human nature based solely on extrinsic forms of motivation, complicated hierarchical power structures that keep people in the dark, scripts that encourage us to put each other down or to work so hard that we have no time to care for each other, controlling leaders who don't seem to care about people—all these and more cast huge shadows. Often the only way to shine is at the expense of the person next to you.

If we fail to give people the opportunity to shine at work, chances are they will look for somewhere else to shine. Eventually, many of these people will disengage from the organization—if not physically, at least mentally and emotionally. Some already have. I must admit that in my own case I grew disillusioned with the organization where I was working. Writing this book and teaching my class evenings and weekends became my places to shine. Shining in more than one place can be healthy, but when we fail to offer people opportunities to shine at work, not only do we suffer, but our organizations suffer as well.

Organizations will not be changed overnight. Much of what goes on inside the organization is deeply rooted in established theories and social structures, and supported by everyday scripts. But we need to start somewhere. After all is said and done, organizations are made up of work groups that consist of people like you and me. Indeed, later I will suggest that organizations are nothing more than systems that we created in the first place to work more effectively and efficiently, which have taken on a life of their own and gotten out of hand. That doesn't mean they aren't powerful, but it suggests that we can change them for the better. And even if we can't change the organization, we can change ourselves. We can discover ways to shine where we stand by meeting needs the organization in its "bigness" cannot meet, needs for quality in our work, needs for a craft or an art form to be resurrected, needs for mentors or caring people to be present for others who are lost and alone in the struggle.

We live in difficult times. Social structures are falling apart and rapid change is a way of life. It is hard to find places to shine. But one truth sticks out in the midst of the chaos of our times. We shine the brightest when we lose ourselves in a special work or purpose, when we extend ourselves to others in need. Based on this truth, I believe we live in a time of opportunity. There have been few times in history when we needed each other more than we do today.

This book is about embracing the shadows cast by our organizations so that we can turn them into places where more people are given the opportunity to shine. It is also about emerging from these shadows, building places to shine, and in the process, discovering your own place to shine. Although these appear to be two separate challenges, in reality they are one. In fact, they are connected in a way that makes our time a time of opportunity. Let me explain what I mean by this statement.

The old organization is being challenged to change and adapt to global competition. The age of information itself is forcing us to look at work in new ways. In the midst of this chaos, the old social contract between people and the organizations they work for has been broken. A new social contract is being negotiated, whether we are aware of it or not. The idea of work itself is being redefined. We have been presented with an opportunity to get involved in the process of negotiating new, healthier relationships between people and their work—and in the process discover our own places to shine. Thus, the two challenges are connected. Through building places to shine at work, we will discover our own places to shine.

On the surface it might appear that this book is written only for people who work for large organizations. And indeed, it is written for those who work in large organizations, but its scope stretches beyond the boundaries of the formal organization. All of us need to discover ways to shine in an upside-down world. We need to learn how to reconnect with ourselves, each other, and our work in more meaningful ways, regardless of where we choose to shine. This book is my attempt to facilitate that reconnecting process wherever it is happening.

I had four objectives in mind when I set out to write this book. I will list them here so that you can check back every so often to refocus on the purpose of the book or to see if I am meeting my objectives.

1. To restore faith in the human spirit and the creative drive in each of us to shine in our work
2. To expose the shadows in the organization that keep people from shining in their work
3. To offer a language and some tools to stimulate the ongoing dialogue and encourage groups of people to build their own places to shine
4. To show by word and example that accepting each other with unconditional regard and confirming the potential in each other through healthy interaction produces an energy force that brings out the light within, between, and around us and helps us shine even in the shadows

I will never be certain that I have met these objectives. Perhaps all I or any writer can do is raise the right questions, offer a language and some models, and add my voice to the ongoing dialogue. It is up to all of us to continue the dialogue. For this reason, I have included questions and extra space for taking notes and adding comments at the end of each of the three parts of the book. I encourage you to use this space to write your own thoughts and to share them with others. If you choose to use this book as a guide for building your own place to shine, these questions can serve as a starting point for an open discussion.

Before moving forward, I offer one final note. It is a note written especially for leaders. This book presents a special challenge to leaders in the organization. The forces of change have already been unleashed. Change will happen with or without us. However, because the old command and control structures will not go away overnight, the process of building places to shine will be heavily influenced by leaders. It seems to me that as leaders we have three choices. One, we can do nothing and let the forces of change take us where they will. Two, we can resist change and fight to save the old organization and the social contract at work. Or three, we can help steer the process in a healthy direction and provide inspiration and real leadership to bring about healthier relationships in the workplace and a new social contract at work based on providing all an opportunity to shine in their work.

For Leaders:

If you are expecting to read another book written by an enlightened leader who has discovered the secret to motivating people, or the CEO who has learned how to create the perfect culture, this book will fall short of meeting your expectations. Or if you are looking for a book about how to get more out of your employees, you will not find that here either. On the contrary, more likely you will find a subtle—at times not so subtle—message challenging you to let go of "my people," to lose control in the art of caring leadership, to put your trust in the potential of the human spirit. Nonetheless, this book is about people and people power. Not in the way we have come to think of when we write and talk about empowerment these days, but in a way that recognizes the power of the human spirit within and between us and respects the unique contribution of each and every person as well as the need for caring and confirming relationships.

I must warn you that this book won't provide an easy set of answers. Rather, you will be challenged in this book to embrace the shadows cast by our organizations and called to inspire others to build places to shine. In truth, the task before us is not an easy one. Treating the individual with respect, nurturing an environment that brings out the best in each person, helping people connect to themselves, others, their work, and even their organizations in more meaningful ways may not bring about short-term, bottom-line results. At least not in the way that we typically measure them. On the other hand, I know groups of people in the workplace who have already started to shine. And they are making a difference in the performance of the companies they work for. I also know some enlightened organizations that are beginning to reap the benefits of a workforce that shines. They have learned by experience that the best companies of the next century must appeal to our hearts and not just our heads. They have discovered the power of tapping into the human spirit. They have begun to appreciate what it is like to work in a place to shine. And as a result, the organizations where they work are shining as well.

But if the results are intangible at first and only unfold over the long run, why should one want to create a place to shine? Although I am convinced that the payoff is there, both short term and long term—if nothing else in the joy people experience as they emerge from the shadows and begin to take charge of their work— the best answer I can give you is that it is right to do so. The future of our organizations and our society in general depends on it. We have the opportunity to create a better, more caring world for our children and our grandchildren, one wherein we learn how to treat our world and each other in ways that ensure our long-term survival as a species.

This presents a special challenge to those of us who have assumed leadership roles in the organizations of America. Because we have power over others—whether we want it or not—we must be caretakers of the human potential all around us. Beyond that, we are called to be an inspiration to others, to bring out the human spirit of those within our influence. It is a responsibility of leadership we cannot run away from or hide behind bottom-line results to avoid. We must be bold, caring leaders who do our part to bring about a better world. We must dare to create our own visions of a place to shine.

Our Need to Shine at Work

1

Shining Has Three Parts

> Work can provide the opportunity for spiritual and personal, as
> well as financial, growth. If it doesn't, then we're wasting far too
> much of our lives on it.
>
> from *Love and Profit: The Art of Caring Leadership*
> ... by JAMES AUTRY

Once when the great Dr. Freud was asked for a definition of
the capacities of the truly mature person, he replied, "Lieben und
arbeiten"—to love and to work. These famous words have been
echoed by experts in the field of human behavior for years and
interpreted in many ways, some closer to the original meaning
than others. I am not about to claim I understand the deeper
meaning of Freud's profound words, but I believe it is safe to say
that becoming a person with a self of one's own has something
to do with at least two dimensions. One is the ability to relate to
others, to give love and to accept love in return. The other is the
freedom to work, to create something, to perform a physical or
mental act, to search for truth and develop a unique perspective.

I doubt that Freud was commenting on the American workplace when he spoke these famous words, but they have meaning that applies to work nonetheless. After thirty years of

practicing the art of leadership and listening to the students in my classes talk about their work, I have concluded that in order to shine in our work, we must be given the opportunity to love as well as to work. And both in the same place. We need to feel that we have the freedom to create, to develop our special gifts in ways that are unique to our calling. But we must also be given the opportunity to connect our gifts to others, to feel that our gifts, and thus our very selves, are confirmed by others who care about us.

There is one more connection that Freud forgot to mention. It is one that I have noted in my conversations with people I know who shine in their work. It is a connection that Mihaly Csikszentmihalyi, author of *Flow* and *The Evolving Self*, discovered when he observed people who seemed to love their work, who experienced what he called *flow*, a sense of being swept up in the flow of their work (Csikszentmihalyi, 1990). People who shine in their work find ways to connect their work to purposes beyond the immediate. Some call it a spiritual connection; others refer to a sense of wholeness and harmony with the forces of the universe. So then there are really three parts to shining: to love, to work, and to connect to purposes beyond the immediate. What's more, the three are connected. In the sharing of our gifts and connecting them to purposes beyond the immediate, our work takes on real meaning. Sound confusing? Perhaps a story would help.

When I reflect further on what it means to shine in our work, I think of my youngest son, Joel. He loves to fish. I mean fish for the art of it.

I recall on several occasions watching Joel thread a line with ease or bait a hook with perfection. He loves to explain to me the delicate art of putting a worm at the end of a hook just right, so that a bass will find it appealing, or to show me how to release a Northern without causing it injury. He is into "catch and release." He seldom if ever keeps a fish. I'm not even sure he likes fish— for eating, that is. I only know he loves the art of fishing.

Joel loves to fish alone at times, but he also loves to share his art. If you were to roam the banks of Rice Lake where I live, you would hear the name Joel Hanson spoken with affection from the lips of those who frequent its shores. They all know and love him. And he loves them in return. When he has been sick or unable to fish for a few days they have knocked at my door asking for him. I know what they are missing. Because I too have experienced the joy of fishing with Joel.

When Joel shares his art he talks about another connection, one that is more spiritual in nature. He describes it as a sense that surrounds him to the extent that he forgets himself and gets lost in the art of fishing. He says that when this sense of wholeness surrounds him he feels connected to everything and everyone around him.

As my son Joel has taught me, we shine our best when we are given an opportunity to perfect an art and then share it with others, "to work and to love," as Freud would say. But he has challenged me to go beyond these immediate connections. He has introduced me to a third part of shining by showing me how to appreciate the power of connecting one's gift to the gift of life itself in a way that weaves it into a larger pattern, so that one's work forms a life theme that connects to other life themes that transcend the immediate. These lessons have meaning for us in the workplace. Our work organizations should be places where people love and work in the same place—even places where people connect to energy sources that transcend the immediate. I call them places to shine.

A place to shine would give everyone the opportunity to work, to care for each other, and to connect to purposes beyond the immediate—all in the same place. In fact, I would go so far as to assert that one cannot truly shine unless all three are present. The spiritual writer, Frederick Buechner, made my point better than I can when he wrote: "You can survive on your own. You can grow on your own. You can even prevail on your own. But you cannot become human on your own" (Buechner, 1991). Buechner reminds us of a valuable lesson we seem to have forgotten over the years. To work without loving both our work and each other, and connecting it to purposes beyond the immediate, robs our work of a powerful energy source: the human spirit.

Let me summarize what I think this means. In order for people to shine in their work, three things must happen. First, we must be allowed to experience the sheer joy of perfecting our special gifts and learning new truths. Second, we must be given the opportunity to share our gift, to feel needed and appreciated by others who care. Third, we must be given the opportunity to connect to purposes that transcend the immediate. In fact, I think Buechner was telling us that we can master all kinds of new skills, adapt all the right habits, and search for truth until we are blue in the face, but until we connect to others we care about and forces beyond the immediate, we will fail to tap into the true power of the human spirit within, between, and around us.

It seems to me that whereas we have done a decent job of helping more people find opportunities to develop themselves and perfect a work, we have done a lousy job of appreciating and confirming each other and connecting our gifts to purposes beyond the immediate. One of the central themes of this book is that if we are to emerge from the shadows at work and build places to shine, we will need to learn how to appreciate and confirm each other and open our thinking to purposes beyond the immediate.

We have been fooled into thinking that we can separate parts of ourselves from our work. We have been encouraged to leave our hearts and souls at home. From a personal perspective, I have learned the hard way that it does not pay to leave my heart out of my work. Early in my career I listened to those who told me to be tough, to separate working from loving, to leave my heart at home so that I could make those hard decisions without remorse, like firing someone when I had to. I even tried to be tough like I was told to be. Over the years, I discovered a truth about leadership and about people that wise leaders and thinkers have been telling us for a long time. We cannot deny our humanity or try to be someone other than who we are. We become whole persons and shine only when we dare to be ourselves and to love and to work in the same place, no matter where we are.

In the chapter that follows, I will suggest that each culture defines for its people what it means to love and to work. Critics of Western culture say that we place too heavy an emphasis on work and status, that our work defines who we are. Some imply we would be better off if we returned to a time when people were defined by their relationships, to themselves, others, their work, and even the spiritual. I would agree with this kind of thinking wholeheartedly, but I would be quick to remind all that work has always been part of who we are—an important part. The real problem with shining in our work today is not that it shapes our identity or that we are our work. Rather, it is that working, caring for each other, and connecting to purposes beyond the immediate got disconnected somehow. We need to put them back together again so that we can shine in our work.

2

Scripts in Our Heads

In order that people may be happy in their work, these three
things are needed: They must be fit for it. They must not do too
much of it. And they must have a sense of success in it.

. . . JOHN RUSKIN

There is a paradox inherent in certain truths. Although they
transcend time and place, they must still be rediscovered and interpreted anew for each era. So it is with the truth that shining has
three parts. Each culture must in its own time define what it means
to love, to work, and to connect to purposes beyond the immediate. Another way to put this is to say that every culture must define what it means to shine.

Some cultures require more individual effort to shine than
others. Others merely require that one be born into the right group.
Both have their advantages and disadvantages. The anthropologist Edward Hall calls group-centered cultures *high context* and
individual-centered cultures *low context* (Hall, 1976). In high-
context cultures, the individual is connected in the context of the
group and valued as part of the whole. Meaning is found in relationships and one's role is defined within the context of the group
itself. Unfortunately, this often places restrictions on one's options

9

to shine. On the other hand, low-context cultures, like the one we live in, offer multiple opportunities to shine (at least on the surface), but at the sacrifice of connections to the whole, and close personal connections in general. In low-context cultures, roles are separated from the context of the group and meaning is conveyed through shared information. Thus, in low-context cultures, one must discover ways to shine as an individual separate from the group. Fortunately, others before us have already wrestled with this issue and established identities for us to choose from, so even low-context cultures offer scripted ways to shine.

One way to describe how people who live in low-context cultures discover ways to shine is to think in terms of scripts in our heads. These scripts get into our heads when we are children. They are tested and perfected in our childhood games. We play at being adults and look for the approval of significant others. The sociologist George Herbert Mead called this the *game stage* of personal development (Mead, 1967). As we continue to grow, our scripts take on broader dimensions. As adults we have what is called a *moral career* that includes past, present, and future dimensions (Goffman, 1959). In the past are significant memories of moral events in our lives, like the time we hit the home run or received the highest rating in the music contest. Obviously, these moral events of the past are specific to the subculture we grew up in. For some people, the theft pulled off in broad daylight is a significant event with moral implications. In the future dimension of our scripts are the great accomplishments we are destined to achieve. The present dimension unfolds as we present ourselves as persons of significant pasts and promising futures.

These childhood scripts never completely leave us. In fact, many people, myself included, struggle with unfulfilled childhood scripts around midlife. If we are lucky, our adult scripts, played out in real life, are closely matched to the scripts we perfected as we were growing up. But even that is no guarantee of happiness. Some experts would argue that those who learn how to continually discover new scripts are the most happy in life.

Suffice it to say that scripts in our heads play an important role in our search for a place to shine.

In years past, scripted identities were found in the family or the community. For example, when I grew up in the 50s it was still common for males to follow in the footsteps of their fathers or other significant members of their family or community. In my own case, I could have chosen to be a farmer like my father or a preacher like my grandfather, uncles, and big brother. Indeed, my intentions as a young adult were to follow in my brother's footsteps and become a preacher. If one failed to realize one's script, one could always fall back on the generic script of a hard-working breadwinner or a dedicated, self-sacrificing homemaker.

Nowadays, it is harder to find an identity in a script of one's own. Old scripts have disappeared, grown distasteful, or been overshadowed by grander identities presented to us by a media hungry for our attention. Many young people are just plain fed up with the old scripts and looking for a more well-rounded life plan based on more than a career with the organization. Michael Maccoby's research, recorded in his book *Why Work: Leading the New Generation*, revealed a new social type called the *self-developer* who is no longer turned on by the hard-worker script (Maccoby, 1988). Other research reveals a bewildered group of young people not certain what script they want to follow. In fact, one could argue that high-media cultures like the United States offer too many scripts without real connections, making it difficult for young and older adults to decide where and how to shine.

In low-context cultures it is doubly important that people receive self-confirmation. Self-confirmation is a way to describe the need to express a self and receive positive feedback from significant others. We feel confirmed when our self-concept is supported by others, when we feel that others see us the way we see ourselves. Being confirmed as a significant self is critical to our emotional and psychological health. This is particularly true in low-context cultures, where the family and the community no longer perform the function of confirming the significance of their members. If we take this concept a step further and combine the idea of scripts in our heads with the importance of being confirmed, we can begin to understand why some people aren't shining in their work.

In a low-context culture where work is separate from the community, people present themselves to others at work and at play in the hope that they will be confirmed or reconfirmed as significant persons with significant scripts. The last thing any of us wants to happen to us is to look bad in front of those who count in our lives, like our friends or the boss at work. Fortunately, most situations contain ready-made scripts to keep people from looking bad. As we become more practiced at the art of presenting ourselves, we tap into these ready-made scripts and receive the confirmation of others. But deep down, we all fear being embarrassed because we missed a cue, or worse yet, rejected and disconfirmed as a person who counts because we just don't fit. Indeed, to be disconfirmed is to be made to feel one does not even count. In fact, we would rather be rejected than disconfirmed. At least a rejection acknowledges one's presence. But words or gestures that send a message that we do not count can do terrible damage to our self-esteem. Experts tell us that is why hollow praise is so demeaning. A patronizing gesture sends a message that our efforts are not even worthy of being rejected. It puts us in the category of "child," which in our culture means that one's opinion does not count. Being treated like a child can be one of the most demeaning things that can happen to us. If you really want to "put someone in her place," treat her like a child. We all know that it works. We learned it from our parents when we were children. We used it on our friends when we wanted to win an argument, with the famous words: "You are acting like a big baby."

In our culture the significance of the scripts in our heads is centered around our work. We are what we do at work. Warren Bennis, author of several books on leadership in the organization, makes this point plainly when he writes: "Work really defines who you are" (Bennis, 1989). Therefore, the ability to shine in our work is critical. Our very self-concept depends on it. Our self-esteem is built around our role at work. So it is at work where we are the most vulnerable to being disconfirmed.

Too many people aren't shining at work. In a low-context culture, particularly one wherein people are defined by their role at work, this is a very serious issue. Later, I will describe how the very systems we created to help us work more effectively and efficiently grew to cast shadows on our efforts to shine at work, and encouraged us to put each other down, but before I do that I must write more about the importance of shining in our work. In the chapter that follows I will share with you some assumptions about shining I grew up with that I discovered weren't necessarily true, and in the chapter after that, take a stab at a definition of what I mean by a place to shine.

3

Not Everything You've Heard About Shining Is True

Our first duty is not to hate ourselves.

... SWAMI VIVEKANANDA
from *Fire in the Soul*
... by JOAN BORYSENKO

Built into the scripts in our heads are certain assumptions about shining. Over the years, I have discovered that some of the assumptions about shining I grew up with were not necessarily true. What's more, they weren't good for me or the people who loved me. In some cases, these assumptions created shadows that kept me from shining. Perhaps you were also told certain things about shining when you were growing up that you later discovered weren't true. I will share what I have learned about my assumptions so that we can compare notes. Together, we can shape a better definition of what it really means to shine.

LESSON #1: SHINING IS GOOD

One of the mixed messages about shining I picked up when I was growing up was that shining is okay as long as you do not do too much of it and as long as you don't take any credit for it. In my own case, the assumption was based on the belief that we are all born bad and can only shine under the power of a just, but benevolent God. Aphorisms like "Pride goeth before a fall" or "Humility is next to godliness" fostered this assumption. I was led to believe that blowing my own horn was a sin. It was being prideful and selfish. Humility was an honorable trait. And too often it was defined as putting yourself down.

I have discovered that putting myself down is not only bad for me, it also hurts those who love me. Psychologist and author Erich Fromm asserts that the first step toward learning to love others is to learn to love yourself (Fromm, 1964). To come at this from another angle, we cannot love others if we cannot love ourselves. We are too busy trying to feed our undernourished egos.

I have discovered this truth in my own life. When I put myself down, I am not able to give to others. Perhaps it is because I am too busy putting myself down. I have also discovered that people who really care about me do not like it when I put myself down. They think too much of me for that. They would much rather see me shine.

A friend of mine whom I have much admired over the years recently disclosed to me that as a child the only way for her to be accepted by her family and community was to appear nonassertive. For her to be an assertive woman would have caused her family embarrassment in the church and the community—at least that was the implied message. Another person I know shared with me that his father would constantly put him down as a child. When he became an adult, his father admitted that he felt it had been his duty to keep "his boys" from becoming filled with too much pride. These stories are all too familiar.

Edward Hall, whom I quoted earlier, observes that the culture in the United States seems to foster the bad habit of putting ourselves down or putting someone else down. He suggests that one of the reasons is that people are overwhelmed by the complexity of the systems we have created. They feel like victims of a culture that has gotten out of hand. Consequently, many people have given up. Christopher Lasch makes a similar point in his book, aptly entitled *The Minimal Self* (Lasch, 1984). He goes on to point out that people in the United States equate heroism with survivalism. Just being able to get by in a complicated world is a miracle in and of itself.

Contrary to the messages I received while growing up, I have learned that shining is good for me and the people I love and work with. It is not selfish at all. In fact, to be selfish is to be unduly concerned about the self. If I feel good about myself, I spend less time worrying about whether or not I look good or whether or not I am being humble enough. As a society, we could benefit greatly from ridding ourselves of this faulty assumption that too much shining is bad for us and replacing it with the assumption that shining is not only good for our healthy growth as individuals, but it is good for the people we love and our social institutions as well.

LESSON #2: I SHINE MY BRIGHTEST WHEN I HAVE OTHERS TO SHINE WITH

Another false assumption about shining that I grew up with was that needing others to shine with was a sign of weakness. Like others I knew, I bought into the myth of the strong, autonomous individual. I thought that to prove I was strong I needed to show that I was capable of making it on my own without any help from anyone. The implied message was that a real man or woman doesn't need other people to shine.

The great Carl Jung once wrote that there is no "I" without a "we." A strong self implies strong relationships to others. This doesn't mean one automatically follows the crowd. Holding strong to your values and feeling good about who you are as a person, as I stated earlier, is essential to your mental health. But values and a strong sense of self are built through relationships.

Martin Buber made the point I am attempting to make much better than I can when he wrote:

> The inmost growth of the self is not induced by man's relation to himself, as people like to suppose today, but by the confirmation in which one knows himself to be made present in his uniqueness by the other.

The lesson that I do, in fact, need others to shine was brought home to me several years ago when I was giving a speech about my book to a group of executives. The audience consisted mostly of white males over fifty. I closed my speech with the message that because we live in chaotic times we need each other more than ever. I warned my audience against taking a tough-guy approach to the problems of organizational America and challenged them to let their hair down and to share of themselves in the thought that we grow stronger by making ourselves vulnerable and responding to the needs of others. As I finished my speech, a dead silence filled the air. You could have heard a pin drop. I remember thinking that I had either lost the audience entirely or they were dumbfounded by my remarks.

Later, at a reception a gentleman who looked to be in his early sixties approached me. I stepped back slightly, not sure what to expect. With tears in his eyes he reached out to embrace me. "For years I thought I had to be hard, rational, and unemotional," he began. "Your words hit home with me. I only hope it's not too late to show how much I care for the people I work with."

These words from a white male executive are revealing. Somewhere along the way we accepted the mistaken notion that we had to show how tough and unemotional we could be at work. We were led to believe that being emotional was a sign of weakness. We are now learning to see beyond this false assumption. Every day I hear a new story about someone who has learned the joy of caring at work. But we still have a long way to go before we come to understand the real power of connecting to others at work. It is one of the most powerful things we can do to help ourselves and others shine.

LESSON #3: NO ONE CAN SHINE FOR ME

As I point out in the first chapter, a strong self is built through connections to our work, to others we love and are loved by, and to purposes beyond the immediate. But it is important to note what kinds of connections or relationships are healthy and what kinds are not. Experts in the fields of psychology and the social sciences remind us that healthy relationships with others are characterized by interdependence between two strong selves. We must watch out for relationships where one party or both are dependent on the other. Thus, the third lesson I learned about shining is that no one can shine for me—*with* me, yes, but not *for* me.

When we are young and still trying out our wings, the help of a wise mentor can be invaluable. Or later in life when the normal trials of living overwhelm us and we feel lost and alone, the caring shoulder of a friend can bring us back home again. But the role of those who care is to give us wings, not to fly for us. Let me share another story to make my point.

I recognized Susan as a strong performer the first time we met. So did her boss, Mike. I can't remember the number of times he told me how valuable she was. Yet I noticed that Susan was never promoted or given new assignments. I wondered why and asked Mike, who replied, "That's a good question. I guess she likes it just where she is."

Not content with Mike's explanation, I asked Susan the same question. After some coaxing on my part, she told me about her dream to work in training and development and the classes she had been taking at a local weekend college program. When I asked her why she hadn't asked for a transfer to Human Resources, she told me that she just couldn't let Mike down because he had been so good to her and that she was afraid he would think she was ungrateful if she asked for a transfer.

Fortunately, this story has a happy ending. Once Mike became aware of Susan's aspirations, he was able to negotiate a part-time situation wherein Susan worked for Human Resources part of the day while she continued performing the critical parts of her current function. Eventually, Susan went to work full-time in Human Resources as a trainer in Quality.

Not every story ends as happily as this one did. Too often people find themselves trapped in a position where their only way to shine is under the halo of a strong leader or a big corporation. No doubt we need the love and care of others in order to develop a strong sense of self, but we must also dare to venture out on our own and create new ways to shine and discover new places to shine. From this strong sense of self we can connect to others in a relationship of interdependence. Csikszentmihalyi reminds us that humans develop through at least three stages: dependence to independence to interdependence (Csikszentmihalyi, 1990, 1993). Unless we grow to become interdependent, we risk shining for someone else or having someone do our shining for us. Janet Hagberg has developed a comprehensive developmental model with several stages that lead to interdependence. Her definition of *real power* as something that grows through a process of developing our gifts and then integrating them into society and the whole of the universe is a healthy way to understand our need to shine (Hagberg, 1994).

From my own experience I have learned that I shine my brightest when I shine with others. On the other hand, if I let someone shine for me or if I try to shine for someone, I end up either living in someone's shadow or casting a shadow on someone myself. Perhaps the lesson here is that we shine brighter when we shine *with* others, but not when we shine *for* them.

LESSON #4: THERE IS MORE THAN ONE WAY TO SHINE

We shine the brightest when we match our special skills, talents, and perspectives to our work. But that doesn't mean we have only one way to shine. To assume that we can only shine in one way or in one place limits our ability to shine.

When I counsel people on finding their life theme, I tell them to imagine times in their lives when they felt lost in their work and they sensed an overwhelming feeling of happiness. I warn them to think not so much in terms of the specifics of the task, but more in terms of the setting and the interaction. I ask them what it is about the situation and how they related to it that made them feel good about themselves. Often, they discover it was the interaction with other people or the sense of accomplishment from doing something they least expected to be fulfilling. The point is, you need to think beyond the specifics of a job or a situation and identify the broader attributes of the situation in order to understand what it is you are good at and love to do.

In my own case, I have discovered that I love interacting with people, performing (as in a speech), and helping people learn how to get along without denying human conflict. I would never have discovered these things about myself if I had limited my search to specifics. In fact, I might have reached the mistaken conclusion that I love to work in business, when the truth is I love to work with people and make presentations—two things I can do in lots of different places.

The process I described is by no means perfect, but it begins to get at a truth about shining. The truth I am speaking of is this. We can shine in more than one place. We often limit our places to shine by looking at the specifics of a job. Then we become frustrated because our job doesn't match our interests or is less than fulfilling. Howard Gardner's work on types of intelligences was particularly helpful for me when I wrestled with this issue (Gardner, 1985). Working with brain-damaged patients, he discovered seven types of intelligence. Furthermore, he discovered that people favor one or more types of intelligence over others. But he also noted that one's intelligence could shine through in many different situations. Some people are musically smart while others shine with numbers or physical feats. Some of us are good with relationships. But the point is: our intelligence is broad in scope and translatable into several situations. In other words, we can shine in many ways and in many situations. I even know of a business leader who uses her musical talent to inspire her division to put fun into their work. Or I could tell you about an interpersonally smart strategic planner who uses his ability to relate to other people to build strong strategic visions and plans.

No doubt we need to be honest with ourselves about jobs that are less than fulfilling. To stay in a job that does not match our skills, talents, and perspectives or to work under an abusive boss is masochistic and does violence to the human spirit. But I have discovered that I can shine in more than one place. I have also discovered that when I feel stuck in a job or a situation where I cannot express my true self or one that does not well match my gifts, sometimes patience pays off. Sometimes the situation will change or an opportunity to shine will present itself where I stand. And even when I can't change the situation, I can always change the way that I approach it and my attitude toward it. Often, I discover ways to shine even in the shadows of a bad situation.

LESSON #5: THERE IS A PLACE TO SHINE FOR EVERYONE

We live in a complicated world. What's more, our world is in a mode of constant change. Social structures like the family, the community, the church—and yes, even work—aren't what they used to be. It's hard to figure out where we fit into the picture, let alone where we shine. It is easy to fall prey to the false assumption that some people, perhaps you, will never find a place to shine.

A number of years ago the sociologist Christopher Lasch wrote a book called *The Minimal Self*. I referred to it earlier when I was making a point that it is healthy to shine. At the risk of oversimplifying his thesis, I think he was telling his readers that when we lose our connections to family, community, and a sense of purpose in our lives, we begin to lose a strong sense of self. This is complicated by the daily bombardment of pseudo-identities from a mass media constantly trying to sell us something. If one adds to this a world that is upside down and in the throes of change, a picture emerges of a creature alone and afraid in a world she never made. Lasch argues that under these conditions, people equate mere survival with heroism. If we let this kind of thinking go far enough, we can convince ourselves that some people will never find a place to shine.

Everywhere I go these days I sense frustration with the way things are and a feeling that there is nothing one can do about it. Therefore, to survive the system, including the latest wave of changes, is considered an accomplishment in and of itself. These feelings come out in the responses I receive to the casual question: "How are you doing?" It is common for people to reply: "Oh, I'm getting by," or "I'm surviving."

In a world of constant change it is easy to give up and retreat to a mode of survivalism. After all, there is little left that is stable enough to hang onto anymore. But I have discovered places to shine—even in times of change and chaos; perhaps more so then. Let me explain what I mean.

Times when things are up in the air and people have lost a sense of place and direction are the times we need each other the most. Therefore, they are times of opportunity—if for no other reason than that so many people need our help. It is a time when there is much to be done, not only through helping others, but also through reviving lost forms of art and craft and discovering new purposes in a world where social structures, including our work, are being redefined. One way to look at distressful times, then, is to think of them as opportunities to get involved in making things better, thus, as opportunities to discover ways to shine.

Carl Rogers, author of the concept of client-centered therapy, dared to believe that everyone he encountered, regardless of how hopeless his or her life appeared, was heading in a positive direction (Rogers, 1961). As a therapist, he saw his responsibility as one of accepting people unconditionally for who they are, confirming them, so to speak, and then watching their potential unfold. He truly believed that everyone would shine if given unconditional support and allowed to connect his or her special gifts to a need in the world. If he could still say that, after dealing with people whose lives were out of order, certainly we can believe in each other at work. On the other hand, should we choose to believe that some people will never shine no matter how much we believe in them, we will create a self-fulfilling prophecy the consequences of which we might not like.

LESSON #6: I MUST BUILD MY OWN PLACES TO SHINE

In his book *Man's Search for Meaning,* Viktor Frankl suggested that happiness is a by-product of discovering meaning in one's life, that to search for meaning only causes it to move out of reach. But did he mean that we should merely go along with whatever life dishes out, waiting for our place to shine to somehow magically appear? I don't think so. Nevertheless, it is an assumption about shining that I grew up believing. However, I have learned that shining does not work that way. Shining is indeed a by-product, just as Frankl surmised, but it emerges only when I get involved in life and build my own places to shine.

In her book *Developing a 21st Century Mind,* Marsha Sinetar writes about *creative adaptive* people (Sinetar, 1991). She suggests that happiness emerges from the process of setting goals and working toward achieving them. Csikszentmihalyi makes a similar point in his book about flow experiences (Csikszentmihalyi, 1990). I would add a perspective from my own experience. The happiest people I know reinvent themselves now and then, without compromising their values or relationships.

At times in our lives, we need to have patience and give ourselves permission to relax, to reflect on our life and its meaning and not to force happiness. It is a lesson I absorbed while learning to help my body's healing process work on my cancer. At the same time, in order to shine we also need to act on life, to set new goals and experience the joys of building new dimensions to ourselves. I have discovered that for me the answer to the proverbial question: "What is the meaning of life?" is this: the meaning of
           ning, wherever and whenever I create it from the cir-
        es I find myself in by doing what I do with passion and
       g it to others and purposes beyond the immediate.

At the risk of repeating myself, we live in a time of opportunity. Meaning waits to be discovered as we meet the needs of a world in flux. Multiple ways to shine are waiting for people. But we won't discover them if we do not get involved and build our own places to shine.

LESSON #7: SHINING ISN'T A CONTEST

"I'll never shine like you do," a student said to me the other day. He went on to tell me how wonderful I was and how important my work was for the workplace. Part of me was delighted with his praise. I love to be loved and admired. Another part of me felt sad.

The prevailing mindset in the organizations of America is that shining is a contest. It is fed by pop behaviorist theories of human nature based solely on extrinsic rewards and win/lose views of the world, a subject I will cover in detail in Chapter 6. But for now it is important to point out that shining need not be a contest. In fact, when shining becomes a contest it builds shadows that keep people from shining.

How many times have you heard the phrase: "I'm looking to get ahead in life." When I hear this I am tempted to ask: "Ahead of what?" It's like we can't help ourselves. We have to think in terms of hierarchical progression where shining has to do with moving up the corporate ladder of success—even at the expense of others.

In my own life, I have learned to challenge the assumption that "success" is the same as getting ahead and climbing the corporate ladder.

In truth, I was shining more often when I was a so-called "lowly" customer service clerk than I am as a corporate vice president. At least then I was connected to the products we made and the customers who bought them. What's more, I enjoyed the group of people who struggled with me to please customers, even when it seemed they didn't want to be pleased. The truth is, the higher up the rungs of the corporate ladder of success I climbed, the more disconnected I became from my work and the people I worked with. By the time I became an executive I had mastered the art of social distancing. I was careful not to get too close to people for fear of letting my heart get in the way of those difficult-to-make decisions. The higher I went, the duller I got.

People I know who really shine in their work seem to have forgotten about the contest. They shine because they care about their work and others. In fact, they are so busy shining that they have no time left over to evaluate their accomplishments against those of others. I have also noted that they seem to enjoy watching others shine every bit as much as they enjoy their own accomplishments, perhaps more.

I have learned that I shine brighter when I forget about the contest. Yes, I know that part of the evolution of all species involves competition for limited resources and energy. But as Mihaly Csikszentmihalyi points out in his book *The Evolving Self: A Psychology for the Third Millennium,* in the long run, the best way to compete is to cooperate (Csikszentmihalyi, 1993). This is a lesson we would do well to implement in the workplace. Perhaps we would begin to think less in terms of winning and losing and more in terms of helping everyone shine so that the organizations we work for can shine, in turn.

LESSON #8: I SHINE WHEN I DARE TO EMBRACE THE SHADOWS

The most valuable lesson I have learned in my own life about shining emerged from the shadows. The lesson itself had to do with the shadows. It was this. Only when I embrace the shadows in my life am I able to shine my brightest. In truth, until I learned to embrace the shadows, I was spending a large portion of my energy worrying about things I had done wrong or left unfinished.

The great Carl Jung, who probably wrote more about shadows than anyone, reminded us that the shadow side of ourselves and life is just as much a reality as the good parts of life. In fact, it is a bit ridiculous for us to think we can run away from our shadows. They go wherever we go. Jung also reminded us that embracing our shadows and integrating them into our lives can be a frightening experience, but it is ultimately freeing. Jung put it like this: "But if we are able to see our own shadow and can bear knowing about it, then a small part of the problem has already been solved."

We fear the things we do not understand and cannot control—including the parts of ourselves that are hidden from our consciousness. To accept this is the first step toward freedom from their all-absorbing nature. Learning to embrace all of ourselves—including the parts that we do not understand and cannot appreciate—can be a wonderfully freeing experience. This is a lesson it took cancer to drive home in my life.

When I was dealing with my cancer I learned to embrace all the parts of myself and my history. I discovered I wasn't so bad after all. Most of what I was ashamed of in my life was stuff I had done when I was only being human. That realization did not excuse my stupid behaviors nor did it encourage me to do more stupid things. In fact, it freed me to exercise more control over my behavior, to stop when I was about to do something I knew was not good for me or others, and to say to myself with understanding: "I am about to do the same thing I did when I was in this situation before, or one very much like it, and this time I will choose another course."

I have learned that this lesson also applies to the organizations we work for. There too, we must learn to embrace the shadows if we are to emerge from their power and learn how to shine. That is why I am writing this book, in the hope that by embracing the shadows at work we will free ourselves to build new, healthier relationships between people, their work, other people they work with, and the organization itself, and open the door to purposes beyond the immediate. But I will write more about that later.

Over the years, I have learned that many of the assumptions about shining that I grew up with were not necessarily true. I have shared eight key lessons that have challenged these assumptions.

They are only a starting point. I am learning more about shining every day, as I am sure you are. Hopefully, by sharing what we have learned, we will shape a healthier definition of what it means to shine in our work. I hope to facilitate this process with a definition of my own in the next chapter.

4

What, Then, Is a Place to Shine?

(Toward a Definition)

> Concern for man himself and his fate must always form the chief
> interest of all technical endeavors.
>
> *. . . ALBERT EINSTEIN*

What is a place to shine? I have already suggested that shining has three parts: to love, to work, and to connect to purposes
beyond the immediate. I have also challenged certain assumptions about shining and shared what I have learned about shining from my own experiences. But these insights do not provide
a concise definition of a place to shine. The truth is, I struggled to
find something short and to the point that would define it in a few
precise sentences so that I could get on with my writing, but the
words did not come easily. I could feel the answer in my heart,
yet I could not express it with my head.

I could have said a place to shine is simply a place where
you, as a unique person, are given an opportunity to love and to

work in your own special way and to connect what you do to purposes beyond the immediate. Indeed it is that, but it is also more.
Perhaps a place to shine is difficult to define by its very nature. It
describes a condition, a state of being and acting. As such, it must
be defined by those who experience it. And I suspect that everyone experiences a place to shine in his or her own way. Nevertheless, one must start somewhere. Thus, I offer the following
definition under the condition that you consider it a working
definition, leaving the door open for you to translate it into your
own place to shine.

> A place to shine is a place where each individual is confirmed
> as a special person capable of making a unique and significant
> contribution to the whole in the presence of others who care.

This working definition contains some key words that begin
to articulate critical attributes of a place to shine. These words
need further clarification.

The first key word is *confirmed*. As I asserted in Chapter 1,
shining is about connecting. The connecting part is essential.
Without connections we are never fully human. We need the
love and care of others to be confirmed as a person. I don't mean
the warm and fuzzy way that we often throw out in clichés. I
mean really confirmed as a person whose presence is respected,
even if I don't always agree with you or approve of your behavior. It is feedback that tells you, a unique and special person, that you are appreciated and confirmed for who you are
here and now, as well as for the person you are becoming, the
potential you have to shine in the future. Therefore, self-
confirmation may be the single most important attribute of a
place to shine.

What do we wish to be confirmed as? The next key words
are *a special person*. This means regardless of where we come from,
the color of our skin, our personality traits, our social skills or the
lack of them, or where we are on our journey through life. Often
we are sent overt or covert messages that we must show that we

are mature, mainstream adults as defined by the dominant culture before our opinions and actions are respected. In fact, one of the most demoralizing things we can do to each other (and we do it often) is to treat each other like children. A child in our society is considered a not-yet-person. Unfortunately, this often gives us an excuse to treat our own children with disrespect. We act toward our children in ways we would never act toward adults. This is something we need to change. We need to begin to treat everyone with respect—even our children, whose innocent wisdom has been absent from our decisions far too long—in order to build places to shine.

The next key words in my definition of a place to shine are *unique and significant contribution.* In a culture that values individual achievement and personal strength, both emotional and physical, it is essential that each of us is given a chance to make a unique contribution. It is demoralizing to work in a place where you are not allowed to express your true self or where you are held back from sharing your special gifts just because they aren't in your job description. Author and priest Matthew Fox reminds us that our work must come from deep places in our hearts and souls. Otherwise, it is merely being worked or holding a job (Fox, 1994). Spiritual writer Frederick Buechner defined this deeper meaning in two parts. He said that in order to shine in our work we must consider it a vocation in the true sense of the Latin *vocare,* a calling, and it must one, touch our hearts and souls, and two, connect to a need in the world. His words are more eloquent than mine: "When a deep gladness in your heart touches a deep need in the world" (Buechner, 1973). A place to shine, then, would give everyone the opportunity to connect who they are with what they do.

To the whole is a meaningful phrase because it emphasizes the need to connect one's actions and perspectives to the goals of the group, the organization, and a purpose beyond the immediate. It gives one's personal contribution meaning beyond its utilitarian value and emphasizes the need to integrate one's contribution with the contributions of others. It opens the door to connecting one's work even to a universal meaning if one chooses to do so. The anthropologist Dorothy Lee writes that when we integrate our work into a group of others we care for we become "twice blessed": once for the joy of accomplishing a personal goal and twice as a result of having our contribution confirmed for its value to the group (Lee, 1987). It is a lesson we would do well to learn in a world where we have overemphasized individual achievement at the expense of personal relationships and meaningful purposes for our work.

Others who care are the final key words. It is a characteristic of a place to shine essential to the other attributes already discussed. Without others who care about us and our work, we have no way of feeling confirmed as a special person capable of making a unique and significant contribution. No matter what people tell you, there is no strong "I" without a strong "we." You cannot be confirmed as a special person in a vacuum. It takes other people who mean something to you and you to them. I will quote these words from Frederick Buechner again and again if I must because the truth they convey is worth repeating. "You can survive on your own. You can grow strong on your own. You can even prevail on your own. But you cannot become human on your own" (Buechner, 1982).

A place to shine, then, would be a place where more people are given an opportunity to shine in their own special way and made to feel good about themselves. People would connect to each other and to the whole of purposes beyond the immediate, including the future of our world as a place to shine. A place to shine would give as much energy back as it takes from those who work there. It is not a place for everyone. But for those who want to do more than "be worked" or just do "a job," a place to shine is a healthy and potentially powerful alternative.

I realize that the definition I offer here is not perfect, but it is a start. At least it is a foundation on which I can build throughout the rest of this book. In truth, my intent in offering this definition up front is not to offer a perfect definition; rather, it is to stimulate critical thought about people and their work.

Furthermore, by defining a place to shine, it is my hope that we will expose the shadows at work, that we will see how we have passed the control of our work to the organizations we work for by swearing allegiance to the organizational imperatives of growth and profits at all costs, either directly or by default, thus granting them power to define work for us and our very identities in the process. A major assumption underlying the thoughts expressed in this book is that until we envision a better place to work, dare to embrace the shadows at work completely, and decide that we are ready to move to a better place, we will continue to be held back by the very fears that keep us from building places to shine. Thus, it would be wise for you to define places to shine for yourself. That way you can own your own vision, share it with others, and make it come true together.

She Is an Artist

She is an artist and her work can be viewed one room at a time. Or, if you close your eyes, you can grasp the whole.

She doesn't talk much about her art. It isn't popular to talk about being a homemaker. But if you are willing to quietly wander through her home, you will find works of art as wonderful as any you would find in an art gallery—perhaps more wonderful. Because, you see, every piece has been touched by her caring hands.

My favorite room is the study where I am sitting as I write these words. The ceiling is hand stenciled with a pattern that matches the pictures and the knickknacks on the walls and shelves. Each piece complements the others. What makes this room so special to me is knowing that hours went into selecting and positioning each piece and that the artist who created it was thinking all the while about who would be sitting here when the room was finished.

A short walk upstairs reveals more stenciled walls with pictures and knickknacks in a perfect blend. Like the study, they were planned with love and special people in mind. Some of the people who shaped these walls are from the past. Their pictures hang in the hall.

Downstairs, the family room is full of antiques and special artifacts. Each one has a history behind it. Their value lies not in their age, but in their connection to those people who once crafted them or owned them with pride. If you ask her kindly, she will tell you their stories.

In the dining room stands an old china closet that belonged to my grandmother. It was special when I was a child, but not nearly as special as it is today—because an artist has touched it with her loving hands and felt its history with her heart, the same hands and heart that she puts into the role of parent and leader.

Reflecting on the artist in my life, I was reminded, once again, that shining is more about connecting than it is about succeeding—at least as we are prone to define success in our achievement-oriented culture. It is about the freedom to love and to work all in the same place regardless of where that place might be.

I know an artist who shines in her work. Like me, she may choose to shine in another place some day. For now, she shines where she stands. And her shining makes those who know her shine all the more.

The Chocolate Factory

I knew the man that owned the chocolate factory. In fact, I worked for him. No, his name was not Willie Wonka, but he was much like him. Like Willie Wonka, he made chocolate syrup, fudge, and all kinds of fruit toppings in his factory. He also loved to give tours to the children in the neighborhood. His name was Herb.

If you were lucky enough to go on a tour through the chocolate factory with Herb, you were guaranteed a trick or two. One of his favorite tricks was to turn water into milk. The trick was performed with a #10 tin of fudge and a glass of water. He would hold the fudge in his left hand and the water in his right. Then he would ask if any of the children knew what he was holding in his right hand. Only the children were allowed to answer the question. Of course someone would yell out, "Water!" To which Herb would reply: "Ah, good answer, but not quite right. It is really milk." With that, he would poor the water into the tin of fudge and stir until it mixed with the sweetened condensed milk in the formula and turned white in front of the children's eyes.

Herb was one of the last fudge-makers to still use sweetened condensed milk in his formulas. His competitors had switched to cheaper alternatives long ago. But Herb insisted that quality would win out. And for the most part it did. His customers were loyal. Many of them had participated in a tour and watched water magically turn into milk.

Herb loved his products. He carried a small jar of his famous fudge wherever he went. He was known to order plain ice cream at the local ice cream parlors and restaurants, then pull out his fudge, scoop a little on top, and serve it to the owner or the person waiting on him. "Now, isn't that better than what you are serving?" he would say.

Herb loved his products, but he loved people too. He was not as gentle with those who worked in his factory and office as he was with the children on his tours. He would call us to his office over the loudspeaker, sometimes in a gruff tone. But everyone knew and loved him and they saw through his rough exterior. Most of all, we admired his love for his work. What's more, it rubbed off on us. It was fun to work at the chocolate factory.

The chocolate factory no longer exists. A large conglomerate bought it out years ago. But Herb's spirit lives on in the memory of those who toured the factory. I can still see the gentle smile on his face as he turned the water into milk and the looks of admiration on the faces of the children. And to this day I know a good fudge when I taste it. The problem is, there aren't too many around. Herb is no longer here to make sure of it.

Three Workers Having Fun

My work requires that I travel, which means that I stay in hotels a lot. Not long ago, while reading the paper in my room, I was interrupted by the sound of laughter in the hall. I peeked out to see what the commotion was all about. There in the hall I saw two women and a man pushing a cart full of sheets, laughing at what I assumed must have been a comment one of them had made. No sooner had I noticed them than my eye caught three men in business suits walking toward me from the other direction. They were deeply engrossed in a conversation. It must have been a serious subject they were dealing with because they all looked so serious. One of them had a disgusted look on his face as he passed the three people pushing the cart and laughing.

Reflecting on this scene, I couldn't help noting the contrast between the three workers who were laughing while they worked and the three executives who looked so serious. Somehow it didn't seem like it was supposed to be that way. After all, getting ahead in life and achieving success are supposed to bring joy and happiness, while working at mundane jobs is supposed to be dreary and unpleasant. Something was out of whack here.

As I watched the three who were pushing the cart, I began to appreciate the natural conversation that seemed to flow between them. I guessed that what was bringing delight to their work was not the job itself, but rather the friendship they found in their work. They were enjoying each other. On the other hand, the three staunch executives didn't seem to be enjoying each other much at all. Judging by this episode, one couldn't say that being an executive with other executives brings much joy to work. Perhaps there is a lesson they could learn from the three hotel workers pushing the cart. Work is about enjoying each other as much as it is about enjoying our work.

QUESTIONS FOR FURTHER DIALOGUE

The Three Parts to Shining

Assuming that shining in your work involves developing your own special gift or work, connecting it to others you care about and who, in turn, care about you, and being part of a purpose that transcends the immediate, which of these three is missing in your workplace? What about your own life? What connections are missing that would help you shine?

How is the workplace changing with respect to giving people an opportunity to work, to love, and to connect to purposes beyond the immediate? Do you notice a trend toward meaning and purpose? Or are we going the other way with our drive to become competitive in the world by cutting costs and reengineering processes?

Scripts in Our Heads

What scripts were confirmed by the significant people in your life when you were growing up? Did you follow the script in your head? If so, why or why not? What impact has this had on your ability to shine in your work?

What are the scripts most commonly promoted in today's world? How do they differ from the ones you grew up with? Are the organizations and institutions in America, and around the world for that matter, giving people the opportunity to live out these scripts? Why? Why not?

What are some healthy scripts you can think of that should be promoted in the workplace?

Assumptions about Shining

What were some of the assumptions about shining you grew up believing in? Do you still believe in them? Why? Why not?

What are the most valuable lessons you have learned about your own shining? About others' shining? How might they be connected?

What can work organizations learn from this?

What Is a Place to Shine?

How would you define a place to shine? What are the key words in your definition and what do they mean?

Whom do you know whose life exemplifies what it means to shine? Describe him or her. Do you know of a workplace that exemplifies a place to shine? Describe it.

2

Why We Aren't Shining at Work

5

Shadows in the System

... I, a stranger and afraid, in a world I never made.

... A. E. HOUSMAN

We live in a very complicated world. So complicated that it is difficult to figure out what is going on at times, let alone find a place to shine. Our systems, including the organizations we work for, have grown out of hand. It is a natural progression to create bigger-than-life systems with demands of their own, according to anthropologist Edward Hall. There is even a fancy term for it: *extension transference* (Hall, 1976).

Extension transference is a phenomenon that occurs when we create systems to help us do things more efficiently and effectively and in ways that we can measure and control. Often these are processes that we once did quite naturally on our own. In fact, all systems are really extensions of processes found in nature. For example, we have taken the natural human drive to learn and created school systems so that we can learn quicker and better and control and measure the output, using the same standards for everyone. Or we have taken our natural drive to work and created large organizations in order to make things faster and better and to ensure progress.

Transferring human needs and basic drives into complex systems may be a natural progression, but it has its price. Eventually the extensions control their creators. Why does this happen? Well, like all other things, systems take on a life of their own, using the energy of those who are loyal or willing, in order to grow bigger. After a while, we are fooled into thinking the natural drive itself resides in the system. Thus, we send our children to schools to get learning. Learning no longer resides in the person as a natural creative drive. Rather, it resides in the educational system. We are led to believe that we do not understand learning; the school system knows what is best for our children. By the time we got around to asking parents to get involved, many of them had given up or become convinced that they did not know enough to say anything. In the words of a frustrated parent at a recent PTA meeting I attended, "I didn't show up at these meetings for a long time because I was afraid that I would look stupid if I said anything."

Another example of the extension transference phenomenon in our lives is the transference of our natural drive to work to large organizations and institutions. We literally drive great distances to work in cars that we don't even understand, because they are better at transportation than our legs are, to get to a workplace that defines the meaning of work for us. In essence, through the phenomenon of extension transference, we literally transfer the natural human drive to the extension and give it permission to define our needs and basic human drives for us.

Nowhere does the phenomenon of extension transference affect us more than in the workplace. As our organizations grew, we began to view them as living organisms. We personified "the organization" and talked about it as if it made decisions for us. And the truth is: it did. Phrases like: "The organization decided to make some cutbacks," "The organization must grow to survive," or "If it's good for the organization, it's good for the people" became hall talk familiar to anyone who worked for a large company or institution.

Once we accepted the idea that the organization was a living organism that like all living organisms needed to be fed and
to grow, buying into the organization's imperatives was an easy
next step—even if it meant giving up other dimensions of our
lives and sacrificing relationships at home and in the community.
Some experts, like Douglas LaBier, author of *Modern Madness: The
Emotional Fallout of Success*, suggested that those who bought into
the organizational imperative for growth and profits at all costs
were the working sick (LaBier, 1986). Ann Wilson Schaef and
Dianne Fassel went a step further and declared that those who
looked like they were loyal executives were sometimes worka-
holics in disguise, addicted to the organizational imperatives and
rituals (Schaef and Fassel, 1988). Ironically, those who were suf-
fering from burnout were really the healthy people. Because in
order to buy into a sick system, one had to be a little sick.

Perhaps I am exaggerating, but my point is this. By accepting the organizational imperatives without question we literally
granted our organizations the right to define work for us, and our
very identities at work in the process. As a result, we no longer
owned our work or our identities. The ownership had been transferred to the organization. In the meantime, our organizations
kept getting bigger and bigger.

In the decade of the 80s many of our organizations went
through a mission-vision craze. We were all told that we needed
to develop one or both of these. Often it involved seminars, retreats, and outside consultants. A story from a friend of mine might
sound familiar.

Karen worked for a large health care provider. Like other organizations, hers had gone through several mergers in the 70s and
early 80s. As she put it, "Most of the people around here have
come to expect a change in ownership and thus a new structure
and a boss every six months or so." It just so happened that the
new team that had recently taken over decided the organization
needed a new mission and a vision for the future. A consultant
was hired and several two-day sessions were scheduled for the
management team to begin work on the project.

The first meeting was a disaster. No one could agree on a clear definition of a mission, let alone begin to articulate one. It grew more confusing for the people who attended when the consultant attempted to describe and outline the differences between a mission and a vision. To make a long and boring story short, at the end of the meeting most of the attendees were frustrated and already looking for excuses to avoid the next session.

I shared my friend's story for two reasons. First, I believe it is representative of events many of us have experienced. And it helps to share frustrating experiences. But more importantly, episodes like the one she shared help us begin to see through some of the shadows cast by the very systems we created to help us work more efficiently and effectively. In this respect, the mission-vision craze of the 80s is revealing. It is a revealing testimony to the dangers of the organizational imperative of growth and profits at all costs.

As our organizations grew bigger and more complex, it became more difficult for the people who worked there to know what the organization stood for and where it was going. The organizations themselves cast shadows that kept people in the dark. I believe it was Peter Senge who said in one of his speeches, "It was like driving down a dark road at night with the headlights turned off." The system grew so big and complicated that no one could grasp the whole. Thus, we all had to go away from work to retreats so that an outside consultant who knew very little about our organizations and had no sweat equity in them could tell us why the organization existed (purpose or mission) and where it was going (vision). The truth is, the mission-vision craze is not over. In many companies we are still arguing about what we stand for and where we are going. And we have yet to conclusively define the difference between missions and visions. In the meantime, people keep walking around in the dark.

I could go on and on writing about the dangers of allowing our organizations to grow too big. If you wish to probe further, I recommend reading E. F. Schumacher's *Small Is Beautiful: Economics as if People Mattered* (Schumacher, 1975). It is a book that was written in the early 70s, but is in many ways ahead of its time.

Schumacher makes the simple but profound point that bigness and connectedness do not go hand in hand. On the contrary, they are often at odds. The bigger our organizations grow, the more disconnected they become from the people who work there—if for no other reason than because it is impossible to understand the magnitude and complexity of them. And the truth is, those in power often like to keep it that way.

My gripe with big organizations is not that they are inherently bad. But they can take on a life of their own and if we do not watch out they begin to cast huge shadows that keep people from shining. And it isn't anyone's fault. It is natural for organizations to take on a life of their own and grow bigger from our energy. But if we let them go unstopped, they take over our work and eventually keep us from seeing what is going on.

If we are going to emerge from the shadows of the organizations, we must first embrace them and understand their origin. To put it bluntly: we built our organizations in the first place in order to work more efficiently and effectively. Therefore, we can rebuild them, this time with people in mind. We can build places where everyone can shine. And we can do it without destroying what is good about the organization.

But how do we get our arms around our huge organizations? How do we begin to understand what makes them tick so that we can rebuild them without destroying them? One way to do this is to think in terms of three dimensions: theories, structures, and scripts.

By taking a closer look at the theories that shape our thinking about people, work, and organizations, we will begin to understand why we are willing to work and sacrifice for the organization and how our behavior keeps us and the organization from shining. A look at our structures will help us see how the hierarchical structure got that way and why we continue to rely on command-control models. Finally, by understanding our everyday scripts, the way we act toward each other, we will see that by protecting ourselves we have created a distance between ourselves and others that gets in the way of our opportunity to shine at work.

6

Outdated Theories

We are a society of loyal Skinnerians, unable to think our way
out of the box we have reinforced ourselves into.

> from *Punished by Rewards*
> . . . by ALFIE KOHN

Theories are funny things. At one level, theories are ways of
thinking that help people to make sense of the world, to talk about
and write about why things happen the way they appear to. But
theories are more than mere hunches. In our scientific world, theories must contain an organized, coherent, and systematic body
of ideas and principles and be tested by science and by time before they can be considered real theories. Thus, a theory of human
nature might describe in an organized, coherent, and systematic
way (so that it can be tested by science and time) why we do what
we do when we do it.

   At one level, then, theories help us understand our world
and aid us in our search for universal truths. But at another level,
theories go beyond the role of methods for figuring things out
and searching for truths. They actually influence the way that we
behave. Thus, theories are self-fulfilling. What we believe influences the way we act and vice versa. If, for example, we believe

our behavior is caused by forces outside of us in the form of rewards or sanctions, we will wait for those forces to tell us what
to do. Our behavior, in turn, reinforces our belief that our behavior is a result of rewards and the threat of sanctions. And so
it goes on and on.

How we behave in our organizations is influenced by our
theories about people, work, and organizations themselves. The
most popular theories describe work as drudgery (unless you are
lucky enough to be promoted into management), people as notoriously weak, but rational (most of the time) and therefore malleable, and organizations as wiser than either the individual or
the group. Even being promoted into a position of power and
recognition, as many of us discovered, was not a guarantee that
work would lose its drudgery. Even at the top, work is still work,
people are still people, and organizations are still organizations.
You won't have to search too far before you discover someone who
was promoted only to discover that work at the top of the organization can be every bit as meaningless as work at the bottom.
Furthermore, at the top there is no time left over to shine anywhere
else. By the time we reach executive positions, most of us have created a lifestyle that demands that we make big bucks. The truth is,
many of us reached the upper rungs of the corporate ladder only
to discover we were trapped there by the golden handcuffs of success. We couldn't go up because we had either peaked out or the
organization had decided to flatten the structure, and we couldn't
go down because we couldn't afford to take the cut in pay.

I am not writing this book to argue the merits of theories
about people and work. Nor do I intend to lament the trapped
condition of executives. These subjects would open a whole new
area of research that it would take another entire book to summarize. But I am concerned about theories that keep people from
shining at work. And I do believe that the popular theories that
have been around for a while do just that. They cast shadows on
people in the workplace by encouraging leaders to manipulate
the human resource and people to become slaves to rewards and
incentives.

Alfie Kohn wrote an eye-opening book about the popular theories at work, appropriately entitled *Punished by Rewards: The Trouble with GOLD STARS, INCENTIVE PLAN$, A's, PRAISE and Other Bribes* (Kohn, 1993). He refers to several studies that show how our pop-behaviorist way of thinking has caused people to see themselves as malleable creatures who chase carrots and run from sticks. Kohn asserts that a singular focus on stimulus/response theories, based on the assumption that behavior is a result of outside forces (extrinsic motivation) alone, dehumanizes the individual. It encourages us to see ourselves as dependent on rewards, while it fosters the overuse of criticism and control. From the perspective of the individual, stimulus/response theories discourage a belief in the inner motivation to create (intrinsic motivation), they inhibit the growth of interdependent relationships of equals, and they can even become addictive. In spite of this, as Kohn points out, we continue to use rewards and incentives in the workplace, if for no other reason than that they are an easy way out. They help us avoid dealing with the complexity and unpredictability of people issues. Besides, in the short term, they seem to work just fine. As the old saying goes, "The quickest way to get someone to do what you want them to do is to toss them a carrot or beat them with a stick."

In his book *Why Work: Leading the New Generation*, Michael Maccoby criticizes popular theories of human motivation at work as *partial man* theories because they "focus on one motivating value (rewards) at the expense of the whole person" (Maccoby, 1988). Indeed, we are obsessed with rewards in the organization. For proof, all you need to do is listen to people talk about their work. I heard it again just the other day: "The problem around here is we don't reward the right behaviors." What this statement says is that we are people who do not do anything unless we are rewarded. And the emergence of teams hasn't changed this kind of thinking. We have merely changed the recipients of the rewards. We now reward teams and teamwork instead of individual performance. But the emphasis on extrinsic rewards is still the same. And the message that people are less than capable of working on their own and therefore need to be guided and controlled, with a nice set of rewards, mind you, but for the good of the organization as a whole, still comes through loud and clear.

Theories that encourage us to view people as malleable creatures to be molded for the good of the organization cast shadows on our natural creative energy, our intrinsic motivation to shine in our work. If we believe these theories, we begin to act as if we are the very malleable creatures that the theory describes. In the end, it becomes a self-fulfilling prophecy. The great sociologist Erving Goffman, who made a lifetime work out of watching people interact, could have been watching an executive at work when he observed, "Whatever he does with his reward and wherever he suggests his heart really lies—(he) is tacitly accepting a view of what will motivate him and hence a view of his identity" (Goffman, 1961). Leave it to Goffman to cut right to the core. By accepting the popular theories at work, we are, in essence, accepting a definition of who we are.

One of the more interesting habits I have observed in the organizations I have worked for in my career is the use of what I call the *3P reward system*. It consists of a pat on the back, a pay raise, and a promotion. If you have been an achiever, you have probably received all three. If you have been stuck in the wrong job where people don't appreciate your contribution, you probably received only one or two, more than likely a pat on the back and a token raise. When I have only been given a pat on the back, I have usually taken it as a sign that I should update my resumé.

The problems with the 3P reward system are the same as those cited by Kohn and mentioned earlier. But there is one other problem I have yet to mention. The 3P reward system encourages us to over-promote, thus creating layers of management that we are now trying to unlayer in our efforts to trim costs from the organization. We drew the mistaken conclusion that the only way to get people excited about their work was to promote them. In fact, if you weren't promoted within a reasonable time frame, you probably began to look for another job. It was a signal that this organization did not value your work or your potential.

The 3P reward system caused me and many managers I know much frustration. If you didn't watch out, you found yourself in a pickle. I remember feeling frustrated because I couldn't find a way to promote a valued employee. Unfortunately, I, and others I know, often created jobs in order to promote worthy individuals. Without knowing it, we contributed to the problem of bureaucracy and hierarchical thinking that resulted in layers of management that disconnected us from our products, our customers, and each other. What's worse, we encouraged ourselves and others to look at leadership as a reward and even an entitlement. When in actuality, as I will argue later, leadership is neither one of these. Rather, leadership is a calling.

Our belief in pop behaviorism and other theories that encouraged us to view people as malleable creatures was supported by the idea that people were human resources. Webster's dictionary defines a *resource* as "a supply that can be drawn on." On the other hand, a *source* is defined as "that from which any act, movement, or effect proceeds; an originator; creator; origin." One of the messages I deliver when I am speaking to audiences in the workplace about a place to shine is that we need to change the name of our Human Resource departments to Human Source departments. Perhaps then we would begin to view the individual as an originator and creator and not a dispensable resource.

The theories about people, work, and the organization that have supported the way leaders in the organization think and act for the past several years cast shadows on our shining. Experts tell us that they are outdated in an information age that calls for intrinsically motivated people to become empowered and take charge of their own work. But we have yet to articulate a theory that truly brings out the power of the human spirit. We still promote extrinsic rewards as the way to get people to work for the good of the organization.

Cursed with an overactive curiosity about human nature, I looked at a full menu of theories about why people do what they do when they do it. I read about theories that describe an economically motivated creature that measures costs and benefits and then chooses to behave in a way that maximizes the benefits and minimizes the costs. I paid attention to the sociologists who tell me that people are not that rational, that we behave in certain ways in order to make sense of our world and that these behaviors grow into patterns that we repeat over and over again. I read about all kinds of need-based theories that describe a creature who behaves in certain ways in order to satisfy basic needs or drives. And at the end of my search I was more confused than enlightened.

In truth, I discovered value in all of the theories I reviewed, but the most important truth I discovered was that human beings are complex creatures that cannot be captured in one theory, no matter how comprehensive. What's more, each person is a mystery; a theory that seems to describe the behavior of one person completely misses the mark for another. At the end of my search, about the only conclusion I could draw with any certainty was that each person is a work of art in whose presence I must stand in awe. And indeed, I do stand in awe when I acknowledge the wonder and mystery of a human being.

In his book *The Evolving Self*, Csikszentmihalyi describes the human species as one that is continually evolving, like all other species (Csikszentmihalyi, 1993). He reminds his readers that we are kept from shining by our genes, our willingness to mimic cultural norms and symbols, and our egos. He points out that we are still programmed genetically with certain ways of reacting to our environment that are no longer as healthy for us as they once might have been, such as our insatiable appetite for food and pleasure that once served to keep us growing but now threatens to harm our health and deplete the resources of our planet. Or our inclination to expect the worst, which might have been a real blessing when we needed it as a warning mechanism to ward off danger but in the hands of a media that loves to sensationalize, has fostered paranoia and encouraged us to think the worst or to feel a sense of relief in the misfortune of another. We are creatures that create extensions of ourselves that take on lives of their own and live off the energy we give them, like the organizations we work for. We are plagued with this thing we call a self that seeks to live and be protected from embarrassment with defensive scripts and rituals. Biological anthropologist Melvin Konner summed it up well when he compared the human species to the archaeaptyrix, the first tetrapod with wings: ". . . such a transitional creature. It's a piss-poor reptile, and it's not very much of a bird" (Konner, 1987). Given this information, it is amazing that we shine at all.

But people do shine. Every day, I am amazed and overwhelmed with wonder by the people who shine all around me. That is why I believe we need to rewrite our theories about people and work, around a belief in the human spirit and the potential for people to shine in ways we have yet to imagine. In Chapter 12, I will offer some new perspectives on theories for the workplace; however, we can begin to bring light to shine on the shadows at work by appreciating the complexity and wonder of the human species, ourselves included.

7

Worn-out Structures

Disorder can play a critical role in giving birth to new, higher forms of order.

from *Leadership and the New Science*
... by MARGARET WHEATLEY

If work is drudgery for most people, and people are notoriously weak, but rational and therefore malleable, and if organizations are wiser than people, it only follows that a command-control structure designed to "manage" the human resource is the best possible structure. Thus went the thinking of many of the best and the brightest in the organizations of the industrial era.

The historian Lewis Mumford traces the origin of our hierarchical structures back to the model presented by the monasteries and the military of the fifteenth and sixteenth centuries. Pulitzer Prize winning author Ernest Becker asserts that our willingness to follow powerful leaders is part of the very nature of the human predicament. We are willing to shine under the halo of heroes to overcome our fears—especially the fear of chaos and death without significance. Becker points out that in modern-day terms, to be attached to the "right" influential company, division, or boss is one of the few ways left to establish significance. To be exact, he puts it this way:

> It is only in modern society that the mutual imparting of self-importance has trickled down to the simple maneuvering of face-work; there is hardly any way to get a sense of value except from the boss, the company dinner, or the random social encounters in the elevator or on the way to the executive toilet (Becker, 1975).

Perhaps Becker's cynical side is showing, but my own experiences working for almost thirty years for over five Fortune 500 companies, tells me that his comments are dangerously close to the truth.

Robert Greenleaf, author of *Servant Leadership*, and a veteran of organizational life himself, shed some light on this issue by showing his readers how the idea of crisis leadership reinforces hierarchical thinking (Greenleaf, 1977). He revealed how in a crisis we look for the most decisive and strong leader to lead us out of the chaos. Often we pick the best person for the job. For example, in the Bible the character Moses was a crisis leader. His courage and leadership inspired a group of people to take charge of their lives and leave a bad situation in the land of Egypt. Crisis leaders like Moses are needed when the situation calls for bold action, but that doesn't mean they should be appointed leaders for life. History reveals that crisis leaders can abuse their power by hanging on long after the crisis is over and feeding their egos with the loyalty of their followers.

Another force that helps shape our hierarchical structures, one that is perhaps closer to home for those of us who live and work in the organization, is the 3P reward system mentioned in the previous chapter. Convinced that the only way to keep people motivated is to reward them with pats on the back, pay raises, and promotions, we create layers of management by creating promotions for our best and our brightest to keep from losing them to a competitor. The result is layers of unnecessary management. I know of actual cases where managers were appointed to lead one person—just to keep them happy.

Hierarchical structures based on command-control thinking cast shadows that keep people from shining. They separate us from each other, making it difficult for us to love, to work, and to connect our work to a life theme and purposes beyond the immediate. They encourage us to evaluate and to criticize each other. They send a message that some people deserve to shine more than others.

In the previous chapter, I suggested that we are obsessed with rewards in the organization. I believe that we are also obsessed with leadership. I have no statistics to prove it, but I would be willing to bet that there are more business books written about leadership than any other single subject. A professor of mine once told the class that people in the United States have more titles for leadership than Siberians have to describe snow—a testimony, he implied, to our obsession with leadership.

What's interesting to me is that given our obsession with leadership, one would think that we would have it all figured out by now. Yet we continue to do silly things like promoting people to leadership, then sending them away to private offices far from the people they are supposed to lead. Worse yet, we have the audacity to give ourselves undue credit for "open-door" policies that let our followers peek in once in a while, as if we are doing them a favor.

The problem with measuring off private spaces goes beyond isolating our leaders. It extends to the entire notion of territorial spaces that define levels in the organization. The size of your cubicle says a lot about your level, thus your power in the organization. I have spent more time arguing cubicle sizes than I wish to record. It is only one more problem with the command and control structures that encourage us to measure and evaluate people and to form layers of people who have control over other people. Different-sized cubicles, based on status, and private offices send a message that some people count more than others or that some people need privacy, while others should be just fine on display on assembly lines or in reception areas outside executive offices. They separate us from the power of connecting to each other and encourage unhealthy conflict.

The movements of our time, like the quality movement and reengineering efforts, are sending a message that hierarchical structures are no longer the way to organize things—if for no other reason than that we can't afford them any longer. Experts in the new sciences, like Margaret Wheatley, are writing and speaking out about the fallacies of command and control structures (Wheatley, 1994). In fact, Wheatley points out an interesting phenomenon. The military may be ahead of big business, education, health care, and other government agencies in emerging from the shadows of command and control structures. The military has discovered out of necessity, while dealing with hot spots around the world and fighting high-tech wars such as Desert Storm (the recent war in Iraq), that a command and control mentality won't work. For one thing, a command and control unit just cannot keep up in a high-tech war. It is forced to trust self-managed units to do the right thing. And guess what? They are. And in a world where new trouble spots emerge every week, the military is discovering it must continue to rely on self-managed units. We would do well to learn from their experience and apply these lessons to the workplace.

The truth is that we are learning, though slowly. Under the pressures of more nimble world competitors, American companies are being forced to trust self-managed groups, which are closer to the customer, to do the right thing. Like the military, business organizations can no longer afford bureaucratic command and control structures and processes. In a way, we have no choice but to learn to rely on self-motivated workers and self-managed work groups. This is a good sign, because it means that we may begin to emerge from the shadows of our bureaucratic and hierarchical structures and that people might begin to shine in their work, both as individuals and in groups. But the evidence to support positive change is mixed. In Chapter 13, I will make some suggestions of my own for speeding up the process and offer new ways to approach structure, but I will not pretend that changing our structures, which in most cases means giving up power, will be easy. For one thing, we must first embrace the shadows of the old structures and admit that they no longer work before we can effectively emerge from the shadows and build new ones.

8

Unhealthy Scripts

Even if harsh interventions succeed brilliantly, there is no cause
for celebration. There has been some injury. Someone's process
has been violated.

. . . The Tao of Leadership

The third dimension of organizations where shadows persist might be the most difficult to change. These are the shadows
we cast by the very way we act toward each other: our scripts.

In a world where people believe that work is drudgery, people are weak but malleable, organizations are wise and rational,
and the best way to structure is around a command and control
model, social distancing becomes a way of life. We become experts
at protecting ourselves from each other. Indeed, we are encouraged
to keep a safe distance between ourselves and others—especially
if we are promoted to management. I would venture to say that at
one time or another in our careers most of us have been warned
about getting too close to "our people." I got the message from my
first boss. It went like this: "Be careful not to get too close to people. You never know when you will be asked to fire someone."

In low-context cultures, social distancing can truly become
an art form. Erving Goffman wrote an entire book about the art

of impression management and self-protection rituals, called *The Presentation of Self in Everyday Life* (Goffman, 1959). He identified several rituals for presenting and protecting the self. One pattern he identified as *role distancing*. It is a ritual I am very familiar with because I completed my master's thesis on the subject of interaction rituals. As part of my research, I observed executives practicing the art of role distancing. I discovered some interesting rituals. Some were designed to position the self above the situation or the role one was forced to play (Goffman labeled this the *aloof self*); others were geared toward lowering the self below the role (a ritual Goffman called the *childish self*). In either case the objective was to separate oneself from the role in order to avoid embarrassment.

I still recall observing the executive who shortly after being promoted was enjoying himself immensely with a group of old friends over lunch. Upon noticing a group of vice presidents enter the room, he immediately began to fidget. When the VPs looked his way he rolled his eyes as if to say, "What could I do? There were no other vice presidents to sit with when I arrived." I also remember the hurt look on the face of his long-time friend who had noticed the same gestures that I had.

Role distancing is a natural thing to do. We have all distanced ourselves from a potentially embarrassing situation. The problem is that our efforts to protect ourselves can hurt others. And when we are encouraged to think in terms of behaviors that are needed to get ahead in the organization or when we see the world as a game of winners and losers, our rituals can do even more harm. They can cast shadows that keep others from shining, or worse yet, cause someone to feel disconfirmed as a person of any value.

Sociologists like Erving Goffman remind us that much of our behavior is controlled through ready-made scripts and rituals that are designed to maintain the rhythm of a situation and prevent anyone from being out of role. In fact, we go to great pains to help others maintain their scripts, unless, of course, they refuse to go along, in which case we are forced to put them down in order to save the situation and ourselves.

Scripts and rituals are part of the theater of life. They are practiced within every organization. Some of them are personal, peculiar to particular individuals. Examples of personal rituals have been noted in biographies of famous people, like the council meeting eruptions of Chicago's Mayor Daley, the film-room frenzies of Green Bay Packer coach Vince Lombardi, or the intimate gestures of former President Lyndon Johnson. Most of our personal rituals in the office go unnoticed except by those who experience their effects. For example, not that long ago a student in my class told me about her boss who made her bring coffee and freshly sharpened pencils every morning, a demeaning ritual I thought had disappeared long ago. I still hear stories about the boss who ritually chews out members of his or her staff in the presence of peers.

Some of the rituals practiced in organizations are task oriented. Often task rituals center around meetings and other daily routines. If we do not pay attention, task rituals can favor certain ways of thinking over others and keep some people from shining. For example, to be a person who cares about people and relationships in an organization that makes decisions based only on bottom-line profits can be frustrating. Too often those of us who are too sensitive for our own good succumb to the intimidation rituals of bottom-line thinkers.

Social rituals are also a part of life in the organization. These center around time-outs such as lunch breaks, coffee time, or the stop-off after work at the local pub on Friday night. If we don't pay attention, these rituals can exclude those who don't fit. Sports talk is a common ritual that has excluded those whose interests lie elsewhere. One of the worst habits we can get into is to tell jokes that directly or indirectly put certain groups of people down.

Every organization has rituals that are ceremonial in nature, like the holiday party, the sales meeting, or the annual picnic. These are often times set aside for the organization to show how much it cares for its people. But often these rituals turn into shallow gestures that cover other, less benevolent behaviors, like the latest round of layoffs.

Organizational rituals are harmless enough. It is when the ritual becomes more important than the person, or when rituals are used to exclude some people or to put them down, that they cast shadows. Most of our put-down rituals are not intended to do that. More than likely we were merely protecting ourselves from embarrassment. After years of research and several books, Harvard professor Chris Argyris concluded that the greatest resistance to changing unhealthy patterns in organizations comes from defensive rituals practiced to keep from losing face. These rituals are particularly damaging when practiced by those who have power over others. Argyris put it like this:

> It took me a long time to see that the "inhumane" characteristics of organizations were probably created by humans paying strict attention to such human characteristics as finite information processing skills, specific cognitive requirements for internalizing skills, and defensive actions learned through acculturation. (Argyris, 1993).

My experience tells me that Argyris is right. Most of the scripts we practice in the organization are performed by people just being human. But that doesn't mean that they are any less damaging. Put-down scripts, no matter how typically human they might be, keep people from shining in their work.

The real danger in ritualized scripts comes into play when our behavior is dictated by a belief that people are malleable, to be molded for the good of the organization. Blind obedience to the organizational imperatives of growth and profits at the expense of our hearts can lead us to a distorted way of thinking. Worse yet, we can become convinced that it is okay, even good for us, to leave our hearts at home. In the words of an executive of a major corporation whom I encountered while recently negotiating an acquisition: "Around here we make decisions with our heads and implement them with our hearts." I think he was telling me that leaders should take their hearts in and out as needed so they won't get in the way when they need to make cold, rational decisions for the good of the organization.

In the early 70s Rory O'Day shocked his readers with an article in *The Journal of Applied Behavioral Science* (O'Day, 1974). His research revealed a pattern of behaviors used by middle managers of large organizations to put down reformers who were perceived to be threats to the system or the career of the manager involved. O'Day called them *intimidation rituals*. The overriding concerns of these loyal managers were twofold. The first concern was to control the reformer so that he or she was not successful in recruiting support. The second concern was to absolve themselves of any wrongdoing in the matter.

The pattern observed by O'Day consisted of two phases with four steps, two in the first phase and two in the second. Phase one he labeled *indirect intimidation* and phase two *direct intimidation*. In phase one the idea was to convince the reformer that his or her opinions were ill-founded—based on misinformation—and thus ward off any further disruption of the status quo before things got out of hand. The second phase was more of a last resort to stop someone who would not give up in phase one, or to ward off a potential movement in the ranks.

Phase one of the intimidation rituals observed by O'Day involved two steps. The first step was *nullification*. In this step, the reformer was assured that her accusations or suggestions were invalid—the result of misunderstandings and misperceptions. Sometimes the managers initiated a controlled investigation to prove the reformer's assumptions wrong. If reasoning and investigating proved unsuccessful in convincing the reformer of the error of her reasoning, an appeal to the organizational imperatives for growth and profits was tried. Or the manager would fall back on the old aphorism: "What's good for the organization is good for us all." Persistence on the part of the manager often paid off. Repeated exposure to nullification resulted in a feeling on the part of many reformers that beating one's head against the wall just wasn't worth it.

If nullification failed to convince the reformer that bucking the system is a waste of time, a second step was taken. O'Day identified this step as *isolation*. In this step, the idea was to separate the reformer from her peers so that her ideas didn't spread, but the more significant intent was to ostracize the reformer in the hope that she would give up the cause and go back to behaving the way the organization wanted her to behave. In the event that the reformer pressed her right to be heard, isolation was also used to create a feeling of impotence. Should this cause her to overreact, her very overreaction was used to demonstrate her psychological imperfections.

When subjected to nullification and isolation, most people saw the error of their ways or the handwriting on the wall and returned to their daily routines. But for those who would not give up the cause, such as was the case with many who brought the issue of sexual harassment to the forefront, another set of intimidation rituals was in order. Directed by the organizational imperative, the managers would move to the second phase: direct intimidation.

The direct intimidation phase involved two steps. The first step O'Day called *defamation*. This step was usually applied once the manager perceived that the reformer was beginning to mobilize support for her position or complaint. Often events were distorted in a way that made the reformer look bad in the eyes of her peers. For example, in the case of those who attempted to expose behavior that involved sexual harassment, rumors were spread about the reformer's own sexual behavior in an attempt to discredit her character and thus her opinions and observations. The whole idea was to use the tactic of *ad hominum* argument to make the reformer look less than credible. Defamation also served to focus the attention on the reformer and away from management, thus absolving them of any wrongdoing or unfair treatment.

The fourth and final step applied in phase two was *expulsion*. In this step the reformer was forced out of the organization. The hope of management was that having gone through the first three steps of the intimidation ritual, the reformer would leave voluntarily. But if that did not happen, by this time the file was filled with enough complaints and letters of reprimand (often including opportunities to participate in therapeutic programs designed to make the reformer conform) that formal dismissal was properly justified and legally safe. And if all else failed, she could be laid off with a group of others in the next round of workforce reductions.

It is possible that O'Day exaggerated his findings or that he was writing about a time that is behind us. But my own experience tells me different. I have seen too many intimidation rituals performed for the sake of the organization. Worse yet, I have watched well-meaning managers conveniently remove a potential reformer or someone who doesn't fit as part of a larger workforce reduction.

As leaders in the organization, we have a responsibility to be more aware than anyone of scripts that put people down. This can be a real challenge, since as leaders we often find ourselves in the shadows of the organization, in the dark on many issues that affect us and the people who have chosen to follow our lead. But leadership is a calling and with the calling comes responsibility. The truth is that we have power over others whether we want it or not. People look up to leaders for self-confirmation and to help them discover ways to shine. It is our calling as leaders to help them shine on their own. But in the meantime, we cannot ignore the power we have over others—even if we would like to at times—or hide behind the organization when it comes to matters of the heart.

I know that most leaders do not intend to put others down. Yet I also know that we do it without knowing. And I know too that it is easy to hide behind the invisible shield of the organizational imperative of growth and profits. Perhaps the blame is in the system itself and the shadows cast by the organization, but as leaders we cannot afford to hide behind the system. We must get involved and help bring out the light that is within us, between us, and all around us. Because this is such an important issue, I have added a poem and a short chapter about putting people down without trying. It is called "To Still a Song."

9

To Still a Song

The seventh of May:
I stilled a song today.

A meadow lark flew up from the grass
as I sped by;
I had no time to avoid the crash.
I saw the broken body fall
as I stole a glance in the rearview mirror.

I can't tell where the bird was going
when I killed it;
I only know that it was on its way
from song to song,
for that's the way a meadow lark flies
in spring.

It will never sing again.
I think of myself, a teacher (leader) and parent, and wonder
how often have I killed an imagination
or darkened a dream?

It is no small thing
to kill a song.

. . . GERHARD FROST

Reprinted from *Bless My Growing* by GERHARD FROST, copyright © 1974
Augsburg Publishing House. Used by permission of AUGSBURG FORTRESS.

I wonder how many times I have stilled a song without knowing it. More than likely I was only doing what I thought was right for the organization. As a leader I know how easy it is to kill a song without knowing it or intending to. I also know how busy we are, and therefore, how easy it is to drive on without stopping.

Experts in the art of song-killing have identified three ways to kill a song. One is to treat a person as if she were a child. A second way to kill a song is to make a person feel that he is just a number in an amorphous mass of human resources. Yet a third way to kill a song is to destroy a person's hope for the future, her belief in herself, and her potential to shine.

There is something about being treated like a child that penetrates our deepest core. It sends a message that we are less than competent, and out of control. We all remember what it was like to be a child—especially the way we felt when no one would listen to us because our opinions didn't count. Treating someone like a child is one of the most effective put-downs one can use. Unfortunately, we are all good at it. Most of us learn how to make someone feel like a child when we are still very young. If you listen the next time you are around a group of children, you will probably hear the familiar words "You are acting like a baby."

We treat people like children in our organizations when we send a message that their opinions don't count because they are less than knowledgeable or not part of the executive club. Sometimes even our good intentions send a message to a person that he is a child in need of help. The therapeutic fix-it notion that people are human resources to be molded for the good of the organization and must be sent away to special programs designed to instill the "right" attitude or change the culture borders on a message that people are like children.

Not long ago a student in my class, "The Self and the Organization," told us a sad but all-too-familiar story about a man who didn't fit in. Briefly, his story went like this.

Al was a gifted strategic thinker in the planning department of a large food company. Unfortunately, Al never seemed to have learned the right social skills. He frequently told jokes at the wrong time or talked too loud or laughed when he was supposed to look serious and executive-like. It got so bad that many of his peers avoided Al for fear his uncomely behavior would rub off on their images. But Al's superior performance and his willingness to work hard kept the organization from expelling him. Then came a change in management as a result of a merger with another large company.

The new management team didn't know Al's work. They only saw an awkward person who did the wrong things at the wrong times. More and more Al was left out of important meetings. He was no longer consulted about major decisions. The student who was telling us Al's story recalled what he had told her before leaving. "They treat me as if I'm just a kid," he said. Not long after that Al was let go. Management said it was his lack of interpersonal skills. But everyone knew that it was really because Al didn't fit.

We have concocted all kinds of ways in the organization to treat people like children—and not just those who do not fit. Making someone wait outside of a private office can put him in the position of a child waiting for an audience. The silent treatment is another way to do it. Demeaning criticism and patronizing gestures are two others. Putting people on display outside of an executive suite, as we have so often done to secretaries, is child-like treatment. Cute nicknames, like "honey," "cutie," and "buddy," have a way of putting people in their place. In her book *Women's Reality*, Anne Wilson Schaef appropriately labeled many of these behaviors, designed to put people into the category of child, as *stoppers* (Schaef, 1991). She observed that often someone in power attempted to make a subordinate feel like a "bad girl" or a "bad boy."

The second way to kill a song, treating people as if they are numbers, has been part of organizational life for a long time. As the old saying goes, "You are your personnel file." Here, as well, a story might help.

Debbie had worked in Human Resources for several years. She thought that everyone, including the vice president, knew her well. Thus, when the position of Director of Training opened up, she figured she had a good chance of getting it. But as the process of filling the position unfolded, she discovered something different.

It started with her first interview. Her immediate supervisor asked her questions about her performance that she had assumed were well-known facts. At first Debbie shrugged it off as part of the bureaucratic process. Then came the real shock. Debbie was told that she had an "abrasive style" that would go against her as the process continued. "Where did this come from?" she thought. No one had ever told her about this flaw, as far as she could recall. What was even harder for her to swallow was the way her supervisor, whom she had considered a dear friend, told her about her flaw. It was as if their relationship never existed. Her supervisor pointed to a letter in her file and closed the interview with a detached smile.

Unfortunately, much of the behavior in the workplace that we view as intimate or caring is only pseudo-intimacy. It is no deeper than the surface. When it comes to making decisions, we are often nothing more than our files. But treating people as if they are their files has consequences. It places a shadow over people that keeps them from shining. It can kill their song.

The third way to kill a person's song—by taking away her hope for the future—is a problem that has been exacerbated by the times we live in. Many of our organizations see themselves in trouble. World competition is having a sobering effect. One of our responses has been to cut costs, including a cutback in the size of our workforce. As a fellow executive put it: "Fixed costs walk in on two feet and they walk out on two feet."

As a result of our efforts to trim costs and streamline our organizations, the security blanket provided by the organization, whether it was ever real or not, has been pulled away from us. At first it only affected workers at lower levels in the organization, but more recently it has hit the management ranks and even executive row. No job is safe any longer.

I heard another sad tale just the other day about a manager who agreed to spend three months away from his family in a strange city closing a plant. His assignment included the lovely task of telling everyone (after he had obtained all the information about the business and its customers he needed under the pretence that the plant would be kept open) that the operation would be closed and that they would all lose their jobs. He did his dirty deed and came home. Upon arriving back in his old office, he was summoned into his boss's office and told about one more job that had to go: his.

Many people are frightened by what they see going on all around them. An article by a derailed executive that appeared back in 1988 in the *Wall Street Journal* carried a poignant warning of things to come. In the words of the author, "Betrayed, vulnerable, I began seeing corporate assassins in the shadows. Predators lurked outside my office; measuring measuring." Since these words were written, many people at all levels have learned the hard way that the organization can no longer promise a future—at least not like the one many of us had grown to expect. Well-known business author Rose Kanter summarized it well in a recent speech that I heard when she said, "We can no longer promise people certainty, let alone a future with promotions in it."

For those who bought into the organizational imperative, the uncertainty of our time is a bitter pill to swallow. After all, these people gave up other places to shine for the organization. Now the organization has abandoned them. In the words of the laid-off executive whose story I shared earlier, "I feel like the rug has been pulled out from under me. I did everything the organization asked me to do. Now, I don't even know who I am anymore."

Some people will point out the justice in this turn of events. When hearing stories about managers who swore allegiance to the organizational imperative only to discover that they too were the victims of its need to stay alive, we are all tempted to say, "They got what they deserved." Perhaps some people did indeed get what they deserved, but I prefer to look at this another way.

No one is immune to the shadows cast by the theories, structures, and scripts that are part of the organizations we work for.

They can keep you from shining whether you work in a new high-tech assembly facility or on executive row. The rapid changes we are experiencing can make things even more frightening. They can complicate our schedules and demand our attention to the extent that we no longer have time to stop and care for each other. They can take away a vision of the future and with it our hope for a place to shine. On the other hand, these times can be viewed as an era of opportunity. As old ways of thinking, structuring, and acting fall by the wayside, we are given the opportunity to think, structure, and act in new, healthier ways, ways that encourage people and organizations to shine together. But change won't be easy. We will need to go beyond the cosmetic changes that we have initiated thus far and address all dimensions of the organization: its theories, structures, and scripts. More than anything, we will need a change of heart. For that to happen, we must begin to tap into new sources of light—one that emerges when each person is encouraged to sing his or her special song—and then combine voices in a chorus that sends beams of light out into the world.

10

A Window of
Opportunity

Any attempt to transform a social system without addressing
both its spiritual and its outer forms is doomed to failure.

from *Engaging the Powers*
. . . by WALTER WINK

I have come to believe that there is an opening today for a new
movement of meaning and change.

from *The Fifth Discipline*
. . . by PETER SENGE

In Chapter 4 I offered a working definition of a place to shine
as "a place where each individual is confirmed as a special person capable of making a unique and significant contribution to
the whole in the presence of others who care." In the preceding
five chapters I have attempted to show why many of the places
where we work are not places to shine. Indeed, the very systems
we created to help us work more efficiently and effectively took
on a life of their own and eventually grew to cast shadows on our
places to shine. The truth is, our organizations grew so big and

powerful that they began to tell us why we should work, when we should work, where we should work, and how we should work. They became complex and hard to figure out. They began to control the people that invented them in the first place. It was like we were all walking around in the shadows, unable to see clearly the dilemma we had gotten ourselves into.

I suggested that one way to get our arms around our complicated organizations was to think of them as consisting of theories or belief systems about people, work, and organizations, physical and social structures that give the system shape and hold it together, and scripts that show us how to act toward our work, the organization, and each other. Finally, I attempted to reveal the shadow-like thinking, structuring, and scripting that got us into the mess we now find ourselves in.

I could spend the next five chapters writing about what caused the shadows at work that now loom over us and keep us from shining. But I suspect that I would end up in the same place Chris Argyris found himself, admitting that the shadows were built by people being people and organizations being organizations. After all was written, I would likely confront the truth that humans have good intentions, but limits to their ability to be rational, that we are burdened with the normal needs for survival shared by all living things, that we are blessed (or cursed) with self-knowledge, including the knowledge of our own death, and consequently we sometimes look to overcome our fears by attaching ourselves to heroes and powerful organizations, or we act to protect ourselves with rituals that can hurt others or make us feel better at the expense of someone's song, that in the final analysis we all seek to be confirmed as special people in this crazy world—indeed, we all strive to find places to shine.

In the final part of this book I will move toward a more positive approach. In spite of all the bad news about organizations, I will attempt to show that we live in a time of opportunity and how we might take advantage of this and build our own places to shine—even in the midst of shadows at work.

To say that we live in a time of rapid change is to make a profound understatement. Business guru Peter Drucker reminds us that times of rapid change occur every 250 years or so and go on for several decades. He suggests that the current era of rapid change, often referred to as the information age, started around 1940 and will not likely subside until around the year 2020. This puts us smack dab in the middle of a major transition, a place referred to by transition expert William Bridges as the *neutral zone*, or more descriptively, as *no person's land*. It is a time when old ways no longer work, while new ways are yet to be defined. In the neutral zone, we don't know whether to cling to the old and risk being left behind or venture toward the new and risk losing our connections and our very identities. In the words of a colleague: "As bad as things are today, at least I know what they are."

As frightening as it seems at times, the neutral zone can be a time of opportunity. It is a time when we can look back and learn from the mistakes we made and look forward with hope for a better world. It is a time when we can make plans and begin to build toward the future. But as we have already discovered, change won't be easy. And it will take more than an instant paradigm shift.

Many of our organizations have already begun the process of change. Some of these changes, like an emphasis on quality, ownership of work by those who perform it and are closest to the customer, teamwork, and general process improvements have been good for the organization and the people who work there. Other forces of change, like the urge to cut costs with massive layoffs of people before seeking the input of those most affected or looking for more creative and fair alternatives, have been devastating to the human spirit.

We, the leaders of the organization, have been sending mixed messages to people. On one hand we tell them that we are all in this together, that we need to improve our processes, work in teams, and drive fear from the workplace. On the other hand, and often in the same breath, we ask them to grow up, to be big boys and girls and accept the hard message that costs must be cut—even at the expense of those we work with and care for. People see through these mixed messages. As a result, they no longer trust the organizations that they work for.

It seems to me that most of the changes that we have been making in the organization come from the head, but not from the heart. We apply the same faulty logic that got us into the problem in the first place. We still believe that people are notoriously weak but rational, and that organizations are organized, therefore rational and capable of thinking more clearly than people. Thus, what is good for the organization is good for the people. This kind of logic makes it easy to cling to our old power structures and lay off more people in order to save the organization, and in the process kill each other's songs. If we carry this faulty logic far enough, soon there will be no one left working or making enough money to buy the goods we need them to buy so that the organization can continue to grow.

In many ways the changes we have been making in the organization have been cosmetic. For example, we honor teamwork while we fail to recognize the deeper importance of stable roles in a work group, or we promote connecting to the customer while we lay off people who have long-term relationships with valued customers. The point is that there has been no change of heart. We are merely putting new wine into old wineskins.

If we are going to change our organizations for the better, we must embrace the shadows at work so that we can emerge from them and build places to shine. This will take more than a few good words and a cost-cutting rampage. It will take a new source of light: a change of heart. We will need to rewrite our theories about people, work, and organizations in ways that bring out the human spirit, rebuild our structures around people, purposes, and relationships, and learn to practice new, caring scripts that confirm each other. Perhaps the source of light that is needed to make these changes is within us and around us, just waiting to be tapped.

As I travel around the country speaking to various groups from all sectors of the workplace about "A Place to Shine," I have noticed a growing frustration with the old model of working and organizing. Perhaps I am merely picking up on a response to layoffs, heavier workloads, and general stress in the workplace. An article in the October 24, 1994 issue of *Time* reminded me again how stressful the current times really are. The very title itself was revealing: "We're #1 . . . And It Hurts." The article went on to point out that America has regained its competitive position in many industries—but not without a price. Many people are working longer hours, some at more than one job and without benefits. Juliet Schor's eye-opening book, *The Overworked American: The Unexpected Decline of Leisure* (Schor, 1991), disclosed statistics that show people at all levels of the organization working harder and enjoying it less. But I think the desire for a new relationship with the organization goes beyond the frustration caused by recent hardships.

Some research shows that people started growing disillusioned with the model of work and organizing several years ago. A major thirty-year longitudinal study of managers at AT&T revealed value shifts as early as the 60s. The findings of this study were summarized by Ann Howard and Douglas Brey in *Managerial Lives in Transition: Advancing Age and Changing Times* (Brey and Howard, 1988). The study involved two groups of managers. The first group started working in the mid 50s, and the second group launched their careers in the late 70s. The second group expressed a different set of values than the first group. For example, they reflected a growing desire for *self-actualization* and *self-involvement* at work. This finding is consistent with Michael Maccoby's research, published in 1988 in his book *Why Work: Leading the New Generation,* where he revealed two newer "social types" at work, the *innovator* and the *self-developer.* Both new types, in the words of Maccoby, "want to be treated as whole persons, not as role performers. . . . they are wary of being swallowed up by work" (Maccoby, 1988).

Perhaps the generation of people who grew up with the values of the 60s are now coming of age and as a result looking for more meaning at work. A recent Gallup survey reflected attitudes that would suggest such a trend among "baby boomers" (the often-used term for those who were born in the years between 1945 and the late 50s). Many of the boomers are now entering midlife. They are not content to work under the shadow of the organization. To quote the Gallup survey: "They (the boomers) are going through the next phase of life-cycle changes: finding meaning and balance among work, family, religion and leisure" (Hueber, 1991). These are the people whose energy the organization is not tapping into. Consequently, they are looking outside the organization for places to shine.

Many factors contributed to this shift in values at work. Maccoby cites just a few: general prosperity, resulting in higher levels of education and a desire to learn and self-actualize; the political movements of the 60s and 70s and the growing disillusionment with government and organizations in general, along with a willingness to criticize institutions; electronic technology that created opportunities for entrepreneurs and made information available on a massive scale; and the entry of women into the workplace. Bill O'Brien, President of Hanover Insurance, refers to Maslow's hierarchy of needs model and points out that many people have fulfilled their lower-order needs for survival and are looking for self-respect and self-actualization in the workplace. Peter Senge quotes O'Brien's warning to support his own call for learning organizations: "Our traditional hierarchical organizations are not designed to provide for people's higher order needs, self-respect and self-actualization. The ferment in management will continue until organizations begin to address these needs, for all employees" (Senge, 1994). Regardless of the causes, it is hard to refute the evidence. People are looking for new, more meaningful experiences at work.

I have noted another trend from my own experiences that crosses lines of gender, ethnic backgrounds, levels of education, age, and other typical ways of categorizing people. People in general, from all walks of life, are beginning to search for more meaning from their work, which they define in words like: "connections," "purpose," "caring," and even "spirituality." When I talk about a place where people love and work together while they connect their work to purposes that transcend the immediate, "a place where each individual is confirmed as a special person capable of making a unique and significant contribution to the whole in the presence of others who care," using my own definition of a place to shine, I receive an overwhelmingly positive response. Perhaps I am only hearing a response to an emotional appeal for a lost innocence. On the other hand, there is growing evidence that people are starting to go beyond an emotional response. In my travels I have discovered departments and divisions within larger organizations that have taken matters into their own hands and are busy building places to shine, with or without the approval of the hierarchy. It would appear that people are searching for places to shine at work.

If you are looking for more evidence to support a value shift at work, you won't have to go further than the nearest bookstore. There on the shelves you will find books about doing things at work that were unheard of not many years ago. Words like "caring," "loving," and "nurturing" are commonly used and part of the normal vocabulary of popular business authors who write about everything from leadership to cultural change. Some authors have even dared to write about things like "spirituality" and "soulfulness" in the workplace. They have prompted the emergence of grassroots movements on spirituality in the workplace. Computer technology has eliminated the barriers of time and distance. People are communicating across company and industry boundaries. Books about companies or divisions that found new life and learned how to involve and empower people in the process are growing in popularity as well. The evidence points to a new emphasis on relationships in the workplace.

We have been presented with a window of opportunity. Work is being cast in a new light. People are questioning the old social contract between them and the organizations they work for. They have grown tired of walking around in the dark. They are ready to emerge from the shadows cast by the very organizations we constructed to help us work. They are ready for a new social contract, one that defines people, work, and organizations in terms that bring out the human spirit; one that allows structures that are responsive to people and purposes to emerge from relationships;

one that fosters everyday scripts that connect people to their work and each other in the spirit of self-confirmation and in ways that bring out the song in us all. They are ready to build places to shine.

The truth is, a new social contract is being negotiated at work between people and their work and people and the organizations they work for—whether we know it or not. Organizations are responding to an information age full of forces, both technical and social, that are redefining what it means to work and to love with changes of their own, many of them struggling to become "learning organizations" that constantly respond to change itself. Again, you only need to check the shelves of your local bookstore to read about what these new forms might look like. But even wise advice can present a paradox. As Charles Handy, author of one of the more popular and informative books on organizational change, wisely puts it: "I now see paradoxes everywhere I look. . . . Life will be unreasonable in the sense that it won't go on as it used to; we shall have to make things happen" (Charles Handy, 1994).

As I have stated throughout this book, times of rapid change are times of opportunity. We have the opportunity to redefine work and organizations on healthier terms. As the new social contract at work is written, we would be wise to pay attention to the fine print, the stuff that defines people and the nature of work itself as well as the structures and scripts that emerge from its pages. In fact, my advice to you is to get involved in the process of negotiating this new contract, if you aren't already, so that you are fully aware of its terms and conditions. If you don't, you just might find yourself walking around in the dark again, overwhelmed by the shadows of an organization that is eager to survive and sustain itself in the twenty-first century and will do what it must to survive. If we get involved, we can become the architects of the new organization and the new relationship between people and their work. We can build places to shine. But we must go beyond the cosmetic changes that we have made while using our heads alone and tap into a source of light found only in our hearts and in the connections we form with others and purposes that transcend the immediate.

The Division That Cared

In many ways we were a bunch of misfits, cast-offs from a system that rewarded the politically correct. Lord knows, we were far from politically correct.

I am still not sure why I went after the job of Director of Sales and Marketing. I suppose if I were honest with myself I would have to admit that I felt stifled in my old position. It seemed like a chance to get ahead, and even be a hero should the thing become successful. I knew that I was not that smart, but having worked for a larger company that had given me exposure to some of the latest thinking about market segmentation and strategic planning, I figured I could bring in some new thinking and look good for a while anyway. I sensed that with a little luck, this assignment could prove to be a step toward a general manager's position and even a vice presidency. In any event, the position paid more than my old job and it would always look good on my resume if I didn't screw up, so I took it.

Our assignment was to take a group of by-products and make money with them, or at least break even. Although I didn't share this with the other members of the division until much later, my personal vision from the start was to create a profitable division that would have the respect of the key decision-makers in the company and give me the recognition that I needed to further my career.

The first day on the job was a real eye-opener for me. I tried to use my best charm, but it didn't impress anyone. I still remember lunch with two of the key managers. They didn't hesitate to tell me that I was not their choice for a leader. I was to learn later that both of them had been contenders for my position. Through this early encounter and others like it, I soon learned this was a group whose members would not be fooled with charm. If I wanted to gain their respect I was going to have to do it the old-fashioned way: earn it.

The next two years were rocky ones, but little by little I earned the respect of some of the more powerful members of the group. I was smart enough to respect their superior knowledge about the more technical aspects of our work and the dynamics of the division itself—the social relationships as well as the task. We still had our problems. "People will be people" as the old saying goes. And we were about as people-like as we could be, human conflict and all.

The more time I spent with the people in the division, the more I grew to care for them. We did some crazy things together, some of them rather unconventional, like eliminating the sales meeting and replacing it with a division meeting so that everyone, regardless of position, could attend. These and some of the other non-traditional ways of interacting soon caught the attention of upper management. I knew that we had made waves in the organization when I heard second-hand that the senior VP had made some comments about "too much fun down there." But we continued to outperform our budgets and thus, for the most part, upper management left us alone.

Something happened to me during the years I spent with this division. For one thing, we realized our vision and became one of the most profitable divisions in the company. We even acquired a small company that grew by leaps and bounds. And I realized my own vision, eventually being promoted to general manager and then vice president. But these accomplishments, as rewarding as they were at the time, are not the experiences that make me feel so proud and warm inside when I reflect on the years I spent there.

Not long ago a friend of mine who shared those years with me reminded me, again, why I feel so good when I think about the division. "Do you remember the theme of our division meeting in 1988?" he asked.

I did remember the theme of 1988. In fact, I still owned a souvenir or two with the words WE CARE on them. "Those were the best years of my working life, because we really did care for our work and each other," my friend concluded. A tear rolled down my cheek. I knew what he was talking about because those were some of the best years of my life too. As I reflected further on the years with the division that cared, with my friend over a cup of coffee, we remembered together the good times and the bad. I remembered crying with the wife of one of the directors as he lay in a hospital emergency room critically ill. I remembered the sales manager who was there for me when I was sick. I remembered struggling through conflict and mishandling it so terribly. I remembered those who had grown with the division and those who had left or been victims of our just being human together. I remembered the theme of 1988—"We Care"—the magic in it, and how similar it was to the magic in the little song about "this little light of mine" that my second-grade teacher had taught me. "Yes, my friend was right," I concluded to myself. "In spite of our humanness and all the times we had `blown it' or when someone had been hurt, we did indeed care."

I learned much about shining during those years managing the division that cared. Many of these lessons I have already shared in the first part of this book, like the lesson that shining has three parts: to love, to work, and to connect our work to purposes that transcend the immediate. Or the lesson that people shine when you let them connect their special skills, talents, and perspectives to a task that fits them. Or the magic in accepting and appreciating people for who they are and for their potential to shine in new ways. These are the very lessons I learned from the division that cared—only this time from a real-life experience.

I now realize that we, the members of the division that cared, were building a place to shine whether we knew it or not. Why? Because we went beyond our concerns for own personal agendas and occasionally lost ourselves in the flow of caring for our work and each other. Perhaps the most important lesson I learned about shining from being a part of the division that cared was that we shine our brightest when we let go of our well-rehearsed scripts, put our hearts into our work and our relationships, and dare to care for our work and each other.

QUESTIONS FOR FURTHER DIALOGUE

Shadows in the System

In what ways and to what extent does the organization define your work for you? How did this come about?

Do you know the mission and the vision of your company? How do they influence the behavior of people at work?

Outdated Theories
What are the assumptions built into the theories about people, work, and organizations in your workplace? Where did they come from?

Do you believe that the best way to get people to do something you want them to is to reward them? What are the rewards you would use? Why?

What are some of the side effects of extrinsically based reward systems? What message do they send about human motivation?

Worn-out Structures
What factors go into the decision-making process when your organization designs a new structure? How did they become the factors?

How do you decide on office space? Who needs private spaces? Why?

Does your structure at work cast shadows on anyone? Who?

Unhealthy Scripts and Song-killing Rituals
Describe the rituals practiced at your workplace (personal, social, task-oriented, ceremonial). How do they affect the people who practice them? How do they affect the people who are the victims of them?

Have you ever had your song stilled? When and how?

Have you ever stilled someone's song? When and how?

3

Building Places to Shine

It is hard for us to think of institutions as affording the necessary context within which we become individuals; of institutions as not just restraining but enabling us; of institutions not as an arena of hostility within which our character is tested but an indispensable source from which character is formed. This is in part because some of our institutions have indeed grown out of control and beyond our comprehension. But the answer is to change them, for it is illusory to imagine that we can escape them.

from *The Good Society*
... ROBERT N. BELLAH, RICHARD MADSEN,
WILLIAM M. SULLIVAN, ANN SWIDLER,
STEVEN M. TIPTON

11

Work in a New Light

The laws of nature do not demand that we inherit the future.
Rather, it is ours to create. We can create a dramatically different,
healing workplace.

from *Who We Could Be at Work*
. . . by MARGARET LULIC

Throughout this book I have alluded to a new social contract between people and their work and the organizations where
they work. You may not be directly involved in negotiating the
terms and conditions, but at some level you are affected by the
process as well as the outcome. As the great sociologist Erving
Goffman informed us, all social contracts imply obligations.
Some are cold commitments, entailing alternatives foregone,
work to be done, services rendered, time put in, or money paid.
Others are warmer in nature, involving attachments that require
the person to feel a sense of belonging, identification with goals
and values, and an emotional attachment to others. In the end,
these commitments and attachments define work, as well as the
identities of the people who enter the social contract at work
(Goffman, 1961).

Faced with a new social contract at work, it seems to me that we have a few alternatives. One, we can re-commit ourselves to the organizational imperatives of growth and profits and do whatever is necessary, including laying off our friends without their input if that's what it takes, to make certain the organization not only survives but continues to prosper and grow. Two, we can just go along for the ride wherever it might take us, accept life in the organization for what it is, put in our time, and find a way to shine somewhere else, perhaps in the church or the community. Or three, we can get involved in the negotiating process and help define the new social contract at work in a new light.

This book offers an alternative to the current social contract between people and their work, the people they work with, and the organizations they work *for*—or if they are lucky, *with*. I call it a place to shine. In Chapter 4, I offered a working definition of a place to shine as "a place where each individual is confirmed as a special person capable of making a unique and significant contribution to the whole in the presence of others who care." In Part Two of this book, I presented a model based on theories, structures, and scripts and revealed the shadows in each of these dimensions that have prevented people from shining in their work. In the three chapters that follow, I describe the way people would think, how structure would emerge, and how people would act toward themselves, their work, each other, and the organization itself in a place to shine.

A social contract based on the concepts of a place to shine would force the organization and its members to put work in a new light. It would address all three dimensions: theories, structures, and scripts. It would take statements regarding the theories, beliefs, and philosophies about the relationship between people and their work out of the fine print and put them up front and in bold print. In this bold print, there would be statements about people and work based on a belief in the human spirit to work and to love, including the power of connecting people to their work and each other in more spiritual ways. It would require the parties to the contract to view people as *sources* of energy as opposed to *resources* to be used at the whim of the organization.

It would have a section that dealt with structures in a way that encouraged cells of people to emerge at the grass roots around people and purposes. Missions, visions, values, and goals would be clearly articulated, but the structure itself would be responsive to the need for people to connect to their work and each other. Self-managed work groups would emerge around projects that were consistent with the goals of the organization. In the section that dealt with scripts, the contract would define behaviors that show respect for the individual and encourage people to care for their work and each other, to connect in more spiritual ways, and to confirm each other unconditionally in the spirit of what Martin Buber called *making present*. It would speak to building trust through intimacy. And it would leave lots of room to practice the lost art of play. To summarize, I have made a list of the characteristics of the old social contract at work and how they might change under the new light of a place to shine.

THE OLD SOCIAL CONTRACT AT WORK	A PLACE TO SHINE
Theories	
People are rational like machines.	People are mysteries, precious pieces of art.
People are *resources* to be used.	People are *sources* for building places to shine.
Rewards are extrinsic.	Rewards are intrinsic; people work for the joy of it.
Work is serious business.	Work is play and fun.
Structures	
Command and control structures.	Emerging cells from the grass roots.
Hierarchical and power-centered.	People- and purpose-centered.
Territories and private offices.	Open and evolving spaces.

Scripts

Serious and sober.	Playful and experimental.
Self-protecting rituals.	Caring, connecting, and confirming.
Killing songs.	Making music together in solo and in concert.

If this sounds like an optimist's dream, perhaps that's because it is. In truth, there are days that I question my own sense of reality. Nevertheless, as I pointed out in the last chapter, there is growing evidence that a shift in thinking is taking place at work. More people are looking for meaning and purpose. Adjectives like "soulful" and "spiritual" are becoming part of the descriptive vocabulary of those who write about work and organizations. Nevertheless, the organizational imperative of growth and profits is still king in most corporations. Change is slow. In many cases it takes a crisis to bring about real change and a transformation that includes a change of heart. And quite honestly, a crisis may be necessary. However, we need to be careful that we do not tear down the old organization before we offer something better to replace it.

When I am honest with myself, I must admit that a place to shine sounds a bit utopian. Furthermore, my head tells me that a place to shine is not for every organization. At the same time, my heart tells me that change for the better often starts with an unrealistic dream. Furthermore, I have seen enough evidence to convince me that others are going beyond the dream stage and actually building places to shine, even if it is only in small pockets within the greater organization at first.

As I travel around the country, I keep my eyes open for work environments that exemplify what a place to shine might look like in real life. My search has been rewarding—once I broke out of the narrow concept that company cultures were revealed at the top and started looking in the right places. I discovered places to shine emerging where people were working with real products and services, real customers, and most of all, with a real group of others they cared for, day in and day out. I should have known all along that these would be the places where I would discover people shining. It is a lesson I knew from working with the division that cared. Once this simple truth finally hit home with me, I discovered places to shine even in the midst of the shadows of the organization.

In Ohio, I discovered a place to shine in a small flavor company where artists still served apprenticeships while they mastered the art of flavor chemistry. While there, I witnessed a group of people who had learned to care for each other and pull together to please their customers and more important, to support each other when pleasing the customer meant jumping through hoops and working long hours. I heard their leaders talk about the importance of family and community. I saw the general manager actually encourage people to strike a healthy balance between family, community, and work. I watched them deal openly and constructively with human conflict. I heard them cry with each other and I watched them laugh and play with each other.

In Wisconsin, I observed a small cheese factory that had thrown out performance appraisals in favor of a new social contract between the organization and people called *expectation renewal*. The terms of the contract were negotiated at the start of employment and reviewed annually. First, the employee was given an opportunity to lay out his or her expectations for work and a healthy work environment. Then, management shared the expectations of the shareholders for the division and the culture within the division as they saw it. As a result of this dialogue, an agreement for working together was reached or renewed, depending on whether the employee was new to the division or going through the annual process of review. I heard several people who worked there tell me how they felt a new sense of power and joy in their work.

In Tennessee, I was lucky enough to be part of a program to transform a sales division from a place to work into a place to shine. The division was in the midst of a crisis. Morale in the division was at an all-time low. They had recently lost the third general manager within a three-year span. As a result, one of the best-liked members of the division (most likely the real leader of the group) had left to work for a competitor.

For several days we went on a shadow hunt and hashed out a plan to build a new relationship between the organization and the people who worked in the division. We agreed to a new vision based on a theory of human nature that promoted intrinsic motivation and pictured people as unfolding mysteries capable of producing far more than the organization could ever get them to do with rewards and incentives alone. We designed a new structure of self-managed work groups shaped by common missions, visions, and values and held together by caring relationships. We talked about how easy it is to put people down and kill someone's song. We defined specific behaviors for improving interpersonal scripts around the goal of enabling and inspiring personal growth while striving for the common good and looking for ways to confirm each other and to keep from putting each other down. We stated in writing the steps we would follow when natural human conflict arose, so that we could learn from these episodes using a gain/gain perspective on the outcomes of conflict. I experienced the joy of harvesting the first fruits of their efforts.

These weren't the only places I discovered where people had learned to work and to love. In truth, I discovered that places like this were to be found all over. I had only to look beneath the surface of the organization to find them. Often, I found places where people were shining in the shadows, meeting needs for employees and customers that the organization in the shadow of its bigness couldn't see.

I learned a valuable lesson from my search for places to shine. Shining happens in the commons where people meet people, where people embrace their shadows and the shadows in the organization, where people struggle with the issues of getting along with others and finding meaning in their work, where people turn common tasks into work with a purpose and practice the art of play. I learned that this happens most often in self-managed work groups that are small enough to stay connected to their work and each other, but it can also permeate the entire organization.

I read a lot these days about enlightened companies that have introduced caring cultures. And I am encouraged by this. But I also know from my own studies and experiences, and the experiences of other seasoned leaders, that shining often starts in the commons with a group of people who care enough for themselves, their work, and each other to take the initiative to build places to shine. Sally Helgeson's research with five major organizations is living proof that grassroots movements of people who care can really make a difference (Helgeson, 1995). The simple truth is that if grand and caring visions are not translated down to the level where people actually relate to their work, the customers, and each other, they are nothing more than meaningless babble. They might just as well be written in a foreign language.

Emerging from the shadows at work and building places to shine is like venturing into the unknown. It demands that we put work in a new light, and expose the shadows of our thinking, structuring, and acting. It may require bucking the system for a while. But people are doing it. They offer insight, hope, and even some practical advice for those who would follow their example. Because they have been there, they also understand the clouds that can get in the way. They have learned, often the hard way, that it takes bold leadership and personal involvement to emerge from the shadows at work. But it also takes a willingness to let go, to put one's faith in the forces of life that connect us all.

In the next three chapters, I will put work in a new light and write about theories, structures, and scripts as they might appear in a place to shine.

12

Theories Based on the Human Spirit

Often our work comes from deep places of solitude. Perhaps if it comes from anywhere else it is not truly work but merely "being worked" or having a job.

from *The Reinvention of Work*
. . . by MATTHEW FOX

In Chapter 6 I tried to show how theories about people, work, and organizations based on extrinsic motivation—mostly in the form of rewards and incentives—and all-knowing organizations that must be fed at all costs have been over-emphasized at the expense of the whole person. As a result, we have lost our faith in the human spirit. Furthermore, I suggested that these outdated theories have been casting shadows, limiting the opportunities for people to shine at work. At the end of the chapter I suggested that we need to re-think our theories in ways that encourage us to see ourselves and each other in a new light—one that brings out the potential to shine in each of us, in ways never imagined. In this chapter I will elaborate on my suggestions.

99

On occasion I have thought that perhaps the best way to emerge from the shadows of our theories about people, work, and organizations is to simply rid ourselves of them—to throw out all the theories based on control of work and the human resource by the organization—and start all over again. After all, the theories themselves were, in part, responsible for creating the mess in the first place. If nothing else, they perpetuated the kind of thinking that gave us permission to manipulate the human resource for the good of the organization. Instead of another theory, I thought, perhaps we need to think in terms of a richer language that can capture the essence and mystery of what it means to be human, such as a metaphor, a story, a myth, or an analogy.

When I look for metaphors that begin to describe the richness of being human, I think of pieces of art, in whose presence I should stand in awe, or wonderful stories that are appreciated in their fullness only after the last chapter is written, and grow to be richer in value when they are shared with caring readers—or diamonds, each with special facets that shine when the light hits them just right.

When I look for stories that express the sacred relationship between people and their work I think of my son, Joel, whom I wrote about in the Preface, or a house painter I once knew who loved his art so much that he cried when he saw spray-painting crews go through his neighborhood and splash a coat of paint on houses and barns that would have taken him days to do with a ladder, a pail, and a brush. He saw an art form dying before his eyes. He wondered who would teach the young how to mix paint with just the right amount of turpentine, not too much lest the mixture become oily or the color lose its brightness. Or who would master the art of carrying a twenty-foot ladder straight up and down without losing his balance. Somehow he knew the answer to his wonderings—and he cried.

Or I am reminded of an artist I know, whose story about turning the art of decorating into a way to shine I shared earlier. When I reflect on people I know, I can think of countless stories that describe people shining in their work. Thinking in terms of metaphors and stories like these, I am reminded again that no theory can capture the essence of what it really means to be human. Nor can it capture the sacred relationship between a person and her work.

What makes us so wonderfully complicated? Like all living creatures, we are genetically programmed to survive and perpetuate our species. We modify and use the resources in our environment in order to survive and to perpetuate our species—unfortunately, even at the expense of others of our own kind at times. But unlike other living things, we are blessed (or cursed) with the knowledge of ourselves and our own mortality, destined to experience the awfulness of growing up aware of our animal nature as well as our god-like responsibility to other living things. At times, we long for the comfort and security of the womb. We are frightened by the complexity and chaos around us and willingly attach ourselves to heroes and organizations to assuage our fears. At other times, we seek to achieve significance on our own, in whatever ways our culture defines significance. Like the character Faust, we are willing to sell our very souls to avoid complacency and the boredom of being satisfied with the way things are. In our need to control ourselves and our environment, we create powerful symbols and systems capable of accelerating the normal flow of evolution, only to find ourselves trapped by our own creations. Yet we are at all times and in all places creatures capable of creating wonderful works of ingenuity and beauty, with a spirit that pushes us to transcend our condition, even our very selves at times, and frees us to care for each other and connect to the universal forces of life itself. How can any theory capture all that?

Don't get me wrong. Theories and theorizing are good things. They are disciplined ways to search for and test the truth. We need to continue to build and test theories about people, work, and organizations. But we should never let a theory define who we are, or rob us of the creative forces that make us special, or take away from us our sacred relationship with our work. We should never let a theory cast shadows on our place to shine.

The 3P reward system that I described in Chapter 6, which consisted of a pat on the back, a pay raise, and if you were one of the chosen, a promotion, cast shadows on the human spirit. If we were not attentive at all times, we fell asleep in the shadows or hid behind the invisible shield of the organizational imperative of growth and profits. We became human resources available upon the request of the organization. We also became its source of energy. Now that the organization is falling apart, it can no longer provide the 3Ps. In fact, it can no longer guarantee us a job. That's both bad news and good news. The bad news is the organization is falling apart and with it goes our ability to hide within its shadows; the good news is the organization is falling apart and opening new possibilities to emerge from the shadows and redefine people and work in new, healthier terms.

The truth is, old theories of human motivation based primarily on rewards and managing the human resource will no longer work. Not because we as leaders have suddenly seen the light and decided to become altruistic in our midlife transitions, or because we have felt the call to build places to shine—rather, because the organization can no longer afford to dish out the same plate of rewards. We are free to write new theories about people and work. But this message too is a paradox. It is both freeing and frightening. On one hand, we are free to negotiate a new social contract at work, to create new, healthier relationships between people, their work, the people they work with, and the organizations where they work; on the other hand, we can no longer hide in the shadows, waiting for the organization in its infinite wisdom to tell us why we should work, how we should work, when we should work, and with whom we should work. That is why the changes being forced upon us are both bad news and good news. They free us to redefine ourselves and our relationship to our work, but they expose us to the light—blemishes and all. What's more, they offer us an ocean full of new theories, but no solid ground on which to stand.

Why is it so hard to wake up? Why, at times, does it seem that we prefer to stay in the shadows? After spending time in a

German concentration camp and reflecting on the lessons he learned and applying them to life in industrialized cultures, Bruno Bettelheim concluded that the three most effective ways to dehumanize a person, kill the human spirit, and ultimately put people to sleep in the shadows of the system were to: 1) treat them as if they were children, 2) turn them into numbers, part of an amorphous mass, and 3) take away any feeling that they might have of control over the future and their personal role in it. In his book, aptly entitled *The Informed Heart*, he warned his readers that, in essence, the systems we created to learn and to work more efficiently and effectively were in subtle ways applying all three of these techniques (Bettelheim, 1960). The very organizations we created to improve our ability to work stole our work from us and then redefined us in the process as malleable human resources, part of an amorphous mass, an energy source needed to help the organization stay alive, grow, and prosper. Our organizations grew from our energy into big, complicated systems that cast shadows on the people who worked in them. Eventually, it became impossible to capture a clear picture of what was going on. So we gave up trying. We fell asleep in the shadows of the organization. Actually, the organization made it feel quite comfortable in the shadows, with a healthy set of benefits and a nice package of rewards and incentives. No wonder it is hard to wake up. Life in the shadows of the organization can be quite comfortable and predictable. Besides, opening one's eyes in the midst of rapid changes and chaos isn't easy. It is like waking up on a cold winter morning. At first the light blinds our eyes. Then we must confront the cold itself. What makes the process of waking up from the shadows of the organization so difficult is that it is hard to see how things will be better when we don't even know what the new workplace will look like.

As hard as it might be at first, we must wake up and emerge from the shadows at work if we are going to build places to shine. Now that our systems are falling apart, perhaps we have been presented with the opportunity that we have been waiting for. If nothing else, we are being forced to crawl out from the shadows by the winds of change. Our organizations are being redefined, and along with them our work. We can turn our organizations into places to shine, starting with new theories about people and work. We can give up our status as human *resources* and emerge from the shadows as human *sources*, the initiators and creators of a new, healthier system—a place to shine.

In his research on people who have found joy in their lives, Mihaly Csikszentmihalyi discovered that these people have certain things in common. For one thing, they have discovered a clear goal that gives them immediate feedback that tells them that what they are doing makes a difference. Second, they are given opportunities to act in ways that match their skills, abilities, and perspectives to the tasks at hand. In other words, they are well-suited to their work. He also noted that people who love their work tend to lose themselves in what they are doing. They experience a sense of potential control over their actions and responses and lose themselves in the joy of the task itself. Csikszentmihalyi calls the experience of being lost in what one is doing a *flow* experience. And he notes one more attribute of those who are lost in flow: not only does their experience become *autotelic*—rewarding in and of itself and worth doing for its own sake—but they also feel a connection to the whole, to purposes that transcend the immediate and connect their work into a life theme that, in turn, connects to the life themes of others. Contrary to what we have been led to believe, that people experience flow in their leisure time, Csikszentmihalyi discovered that people experience flow most often while expressing themselves in their work. The notion that we must have time off to enjoy ourselves and that we find our joy in leisure is a modern-day myth. Real joy is a by-product of losing ourselves in work we love, with others who confirm our special gifts. In truth, people shine in their work—all the more reason for building places to shine.

I believe that one of the reasons that we have come to believe that joy is found in leisure time rather than in work is that we have allowed the organization to treat us like human resources, turning work into drudgery, a "have to" that makes us feel we have no control over it and convinces us that the organization, with its leaders and experts, is better equipped to define our work for us than we are for ourselves. In the hands of the organization, the joy has been taken out of our work. It is now up to us to put the joy back into our work.

Michael Maccoby says that the strongest motivators to work are self-expression, hope, and the flip side of hope, fear (Maccoby, 1988). We have been tapping into the fear side for too long. If we are going to tap into the human spirit, the natural human drive to work, to love, and to connect to purposes that transcend the immediate, we must build a set of bigger theories. But we must never let these theories limit our potential to shine. Rather, our theories must be defined by people absorbed in doing what they love with others whom they care about.

As you have probably guessed by now, I am not going to offer you a new theory about people and work. Rather, I offer you a challenge to write your own theories, based on a belief in the human spirit, the innate creative force in all of us to work and to love and to transcend ourselves now and then in the process. And I will remind you that if you don't write your own theories, the new organizations that emerge from the rubble of the old ones will write them for you, just as the old organization did, because organizations do that. Hidden in the fine print of the new social contract are obligations and assumptions about people and what they will commit to and grow attached to. We must pay attention and read the fine print. More important, we must get involved, rewrite the fine print in bold letters for all to see and in ways that bring out the mystery and power of the human spirit, and return joy to our work. We must write a new social contract based on the knowledge that people are unfolding mysteries, with unlimited potential that cannot be captured by a single theory.

13

Structures around People and Purposes

> Unstructured freedom, whether fenced in or not, is still namby-pamby. The limits must have the character of a skeleton.
>
> from *Freedom and Culture*
> . . . by DOROTHY LEE

What will the new structures of the organization look like under the terms of the new social contract at work? No one really knows, but experts on organizational change like Charles Handy give us some hints (Handy, 1994). Handy cites trends that already point toward structures consisting of a leaner staff of highly trained and dedicated corporate executives who are willing to put up with a fast-paced world, teams of technically skilled workers, a large group of service providers who work on their own or for smaller companies, some who will be "portfolio people" who offer a menu of services, and a large labor pool that will work part-time or move in and out of the system, going from one job to another, mostly in the service sector. Robert Reich divides the new workforce into three categories: 1) routine operators who work on automated assembly teams, operate cash registers, and put data onto disks, 2) personal service providers in restaurants, hospitals, and security firms, and 3) symbolic analysts who deal with numbers, ideas, problems, and words, as managers, consultants, doctors, teachers, journalists, financial analysts, and lawyers (Reich, 1991). If we can draw one sure conclusion from reading about, reflecting on, and observing the new forms of work and the new ways to structure organizations, perhaps it is this. The era of stable work structures and climbing the corporate ladder of success is a thing of the past.

As I pointed out in Chapter 7, the structures that gave form and shape to the old social contract at work were consistent with the theories about people, work, and the role of organizations. They were command and control structures, complete with layers of supervisors and managers to keep people on track and bring them back should they deviate from the norms. In fact, one of the consequences of the 3P reward system was more managers and fewer non-managers. Everybody was a "leader." To be someone who merely loved her work was to risk being labeled an underachiever. For example, in the divisions that I worked for between the years 1965 and 1990, the number of managers grew at more than twice the rate of people in the total division. As a result, in two of the divisions, the ratio of managers to non-managers was less than five to one. I know of one division of a major company where everyone was a manager.

Now, all that has changed. Organizations are moving to flatter structures with fewer formal managers, but not without causing damage to the self-concept of many who were told that to be significant one must move up the corporate ladder of success. The challenge facing leaders of the organizations of the future is to design structures that respond to the need for flatter, lower-cost, yet more customer-responsive structures, while at the same time giving people a reason to want to work in them. It seems to me that we must go back to what turns people on in the first place and design structures that tap into the more powerful, intrinsic motivators of the human spirit: the joy of expressing oneself by connecting one's own special gifts to one's work and sharing that joy with others who care. We must build places where each individual is confirmed as a special person capable of making a unique and significant contribution to the whole in the presence of others who care. In other words, we must structure places to shine.

Research on small, task-oriented groups has shown that people identify with and give their energy to a rather small group of others. In fact, research on combat troops as far back as World War I showed that people gave their lives for a small group of others—and not necessarily for the American flag or some other abstract notion or ideology, as many people assumed. The early studies of work groups, like the well-publicized Hawthorne studies at General Electric, revealed the power of informal group norms in the workplace. One group in those studies agreed to limit production, in spite of the perks offered by the organization to produce more, in order to protect the jobs of its members (Olmsted and Hare, 1978). The power of belonging to a small but select group of others is well documented. This evidence prompted some experts on organizational structure, like E. F. Schumacher, author of *Small Is Beautiful,* to advocate a return to a more decentralized structure of small but powerful work groups like the ones that started back in the late 60s and early 70s, long before teams and quality movements became a fad (Schumacher, 1975).

Jessica Lipnack and Jeffrey Stamps shed some light on the whole issue of structures in their book *The TeamNet Factor* (Lipnack and Stamps, 1993). They start with a reminder that structures evolve. Like other things that evolve, the old forms never completely go away. Rather, new forms are layered on top of older forms and often produce hybrids. For example, the small group structures of nomadic cultures are still very much a part of the modern organization. But then, so are the hierarchies of the agricultural era and the belief in the divine right of rulers, as well as the more complex bureaucratic structures of the industrial era. Now, we have added cross-functional teams and networks to the list. In the end, all we have done is layered another form on top of the old structures. The lure of the small group and the power of the hierarchy are still with us, competing for our attention.

Lipnack and Stamps also warn their readers to avoid throwing out one structure in an effort to replace it with another, better structure before thinking this through. They warn us against throwing out the baby with the bath water. Even if it were possible, merely replacing one structure with another may not be desirable. Each structure had its own purpose for its own time. For example, the small group structure of the nomadic era was great for connecting and intimacy, but it often placed power in the hands of one person, and if that person was less than benevolent, the results could be unhealthy for the rest of the group. Or in the case of the hierarchy, control was achieved, but often at the expense of the human spirit. Bureaucracies brought order, discipline, and planning at the expense of the ownership of our work and closer relationships to each other. Teams and networks may bring back innovation and promote connecting, at least on the surface, but unless they borrow discipline and strategy from our bureaucracies, they will fall short of achieving their full potential.

Not everything about hierarchies and bureaucracies is dysfunctional, but as I pointed out in Chapter 7, structures based on command and control thinking and extrinsic reward programs designed to steer and control the human resource make us dependent on the system and separate us from our work and each other. Territorial spaces based on levels and status alienate us even more. Any time our structures send messages that some people count more than others or that some people need privacy, while others should be content with an open desk where they can be watched constantly as if they were on display, are damaging to the human spirit. They cast shadows that keep people from shining.

Margaret Wheatley offers a provocative view of leadership, as well as organizational structures, in her book *Leadership and the New Science* (Wheatley, 1994). She suggests that the old command and control paradigm that shaped organizational structures was based on a limited and outdated scientific view of the world. This view was based on the Newtonian paradigm that said that matter is composed of things. It reinforced cause-and-effect thinking and encouraged us to break things apart and put them into functions and roles to serve a machine-like organization. Indeed, the dominant metaphor was the machine, and this view extended to people (the human resource) as well as things.

Wheatley suggests that it is time for a new world view, one based on the new physics of chaos theory. In this new paradigm, organizations are viewed as living entities that take shape as people connect to purposes and goals and interact with each other around trusting—even loving—relationships. Order is maintained through self-reflection. Shared histories, shared visions, and shared values take the place of command and control structures. Under this paradigm, organizations create the conditions for organizing, as opposed to the old command and control view, where organizations dictated structure from the top down. Wheatley points to Gore Associates, manufacturers of GoreTex®, as a model organization for the new structure, with its open *lattice organization*, where almost every employee is an "associate" and roles and structure are created from the needs of the task and the interests of the people. Organizations like Gore Associates still believe in the importance of structure. In Dorothy Lee's words, which opened this chapter, "Unstructured freedom, whether fenced in or not, is still namby-pamby" (Lee, 1987). But structure emerges from people connecting to purposes and other people. It is held together by visions, principles, and values. It has the character of a skeleton and not a fence.

Sally Helgeson's new book summarizes real-life research conducted in five successful companies in industry, health care, and the media that demonstrates the power of cross-functional groups emerging from the grass roots (Helgeson, 1995). She calls them *webs of inclusion*. She points out that their success was influenced by the freedom they had to connect to purposes, customers, and each other.

Some might argue that the new, more fluid view of organizational structure based on self-organizing principles is not for every organization. In fact, contingency theorists like Charles Perrow argue there is no "right" structure for every organization (Perrow, 1986). Contingency design advocates like Perrow point out that what works for a high-tech widget factory would stifle creativity in an advertising agency. Organizational design expert Jay Galbraith also offers a more balanced perspective in his new book (Galbraith, 1995). He admonishes managers to become *decision shapers* rather than *decision makers*. He presents a model based on the forces of strategy, structure, processes, rewards, and people. But he too points out that the most important issue to consider in organizational design is how to connect people to the purpose of the organization, the task at hand, the people they work with, and the customers they serve. He warns against following the latest fad just because others are doing it.

Regardless of how the organizational structure gets put together, the same principles of organizing apply to every organization. One of these is that if we are going to tap into the human energy needed to emerge from the shadows that keep people from shining in their work, we will need to rethink the way in which we design structure toward ways that connect people to their work, each other, their customers, and purposes that transcend the immediate.

At the risk of regressing back to Chapter 7, I will make one more point about the shadows cast by the structures of our organizations. One of the most demoralizing features of our functional structures was their propensity to put jobs and people into categories and boxes and then expect them to perform. As a result, many people found themselves stuck in the wrong job. Few things in life are more frustrating than feeling stuck in the wrong job. In response to feeling stuck, we either internalize our frustration and give up in defeat, or externalize it at scapegoats whom we can blame for the fix we are in. Eventually, people who see no way out of a stifling routine disengage; they fall asleep in the shadows of the organization. Some find ways to shine outside of the organization; others give up and lose themselves in alcohol or some other form of drug-induced relief; still others stay so busy that they don't have to think about it. If our organizations are going to appeal to people and begin to tap into the human spirit, we must rid them of structures that keep people in boxes.

In Part One of this book I suggested that there are three dimensions to shining. One is the sheer joy of expressing oneself through a special work; the second is the energy generated by connecting our work to others who care; the third is the connection to purposes that transcend the immediate. If our structures at work are going to promote shining, they must address all three dimensions. Mihaly Csikszentmihalyi echoed this three-part theme in his books. He called it the need to *differentiate*, to express oneself in a unique and significant way, and to *integrate*, to connect one's self-expression to others and to a universal life force, thus creating a life theme that transcends the current task (Csikszentmihalyi, 1990, 1993). He discovered that people find flow in their work when they are given the opportunity to connect who they are with what they do and then share the joy of their work with others and a life theme that transcends the immediate and connects to the flow of evolution itself.

What simple lesson can we learn form all this? Perhaps it is this. We can learn to structure the work environment in ways that give people the opportunity to match their special talents, skills, and perspectives to the needs of the task, and then give them the opportunity to share them with others and connect to purposes beyond the immediate. In order to connect people with purposes and each other, it helps to have a clear purpose and vision in the first place, one that appeals to both the head and the heart—something worth connecting to. It also helps to have well-articulated goals that people can connect to so that they can experience the intrinsic rewards of seeing the results of their efforts. In addition, we need to give people longer-range visions that transcend profits and short-term shareholder value. We need to give people something worth believing in.

A new social contract is being negotiated at work. As a result, new structures are already taking shape. Teams and networks have been added to work groups, hierarchies, and bureaucracies. In reality, there is no one consistent form of organizational structure, not like there used to be, anyway. Old structures are competing with new forms, leaving people confused in the middle of it all.

Stable work groups are a thing of the past. Many people are working out of their homes or in part-time jobs. Those who remain in the organization are expected to run from team to team and somehow still find ways to connect to people and purposes. In truth, it is hard to find work at all, let alone work with meaning and purpose. We are being forced to invent new ways to connect.

As I have asserted throughout this book, opportunities emerge from times of change and uncertainty. As leaders in the organization struggle to define new structures and people look for ways to connect to their work, we can join in the dialogue and the building process and make certain that new structures recognize the need for people to shine in their work. We can demonstrate through our efforts in our own departments, work groups, or divisions that the best structures emerge from people connecting to their work and each other. Some people call this building community in the workplace. When I speak to audiences in the organization, I discover that almost everyone can identify with the idea of building community in the workplace. This tells me that they have experienced what I am trying to describe sometime in their life. Unfortunately, it was often in a setting outside of work at a seminar or a retreat.

Not long ago I participated in a training seminar that was part of an introduction to quality in the workplace. The facilitator of the seminar broke us into small groups of seven people. Each group was given a project or a product to produce and told to create a vision and to design a process to produce the product to certain prescribed specifications. Our group was told to make hearing aids. The idea was to teach us how to improve our processes in ways that simplified them while at the same time encouraging us to continually improve our quality. Something magical happened in our group. First, we agreed on a vision of "creating a smaller, more noise-sensitive hearing aid." We discussed why smaller hearing aids are important to the users and how good it would feel to be involved in a purpose like this. We worked together on the design of our product. We set up a production team and talked about matching skills and interests to roles in the production, distribution, marketing, and selling of the product. We interviewed our customers and listened to their needs and wishes. We actually had fun doing it. And in the process of doing all this, we connected to each other. Unfortunately, when we returned to work after two wonderful days and attempted to apply what we had learned, we soon discovered that nothing had changed while we were gone. We immediately bumped up against the same structural barriers that existed before we were sent away to our seminar.

Translating community-like work experiences into the organization seldom works. The shadows of the hierarchical structure won't permit it. Nevertheless, new structures can emerge if we let them. Csikszentmihalyi even suggests a model for doing it, what he calls a *cell* consisting of a small group of five to seven people who take ownership of an issue or a task. Within this cell four roles emerge: 1) a gatherer of information about the issue or task, 2) a coordinator of activities with other groups in the system to ensure that the goals of the group are consistent with the goals of the greater organization, 3) someone who is interested in facilitating and coordinating what needs to get done, while promoting harmony and cooperation in the group, and 4) someone whose interests lie in maintaining the group's values and beliefs, which give it hope, identity, and purpose (Csikszentmihalyi, 1993). Ernest Bormann offers another model, based on small-group research on norms and roles emerging from a process called *symbolic convergence*. It is a process wherein self-managed groups are allowed to define common purposes and visions and discover meaningful roles that help them learn and grow as individuals, while at the same time they connect personal growth to common goals for the good of the group as a whole (Bormann, 1990).

M. Scott Peck offers a model of community building in the workplace that encourages people to go through the sometimes painful process of embracing the shadows in their efforts to build real community (Peck, 1987). Peck's model describes four phases of community building: 1) pseudocommunity, 2) chaos, 3) emptiness, and 4) community. In phase one, we pretend to be one happy family, but often avoid true intimacy and ignore sensitive issues just to keep a false peace. If we dare to go below the surface to be intimate with each other and deal with sensitive issues like the natural human conflict that emerges from working together and discovering meaningful roles for ourselves and each other, we move to phase 2 and experience chaos for awhile. In phase three, according to Peck, we have two choices. One, we can choose to move to organization and make rules to avoid further intimacy, or two, we can empty ourselves of preconceived notions about people and work and move to phase 4: community. Only by going through the difficult task of embracing the shadows of our own "humanness" can we move to real connections to our work and each other. Both Peck and Bormann describe becoming a work group community as a conversion process whereby people move from a focus on the individual to a focus on the individual as well as the group; one might say, from "me" to "we," without losing "me" or "you" in the process.

Experts are offering us healthier alternatives from which to build structure in the new organizations of the twenty-first century. But the important thing is not the structure itself. The important thing is to get everyone involved so that people take ownership of the process and begin to experience the joy of building a work community by connecting to their work, each other, and purposes worth working for—even if this means that we must build work communities that extend beyond the traditional boundaries of the organization and reach out to our communities and into our homes. In order to connect people to their work and each other, we must do more than align personal vision with corporate visions. We must give people the opportunity to own the process of building structures around shared visions, values, and meaning, whereby shared goals emerge that help both people and organizations learn and grow. If we allow structures to emerge around purposes and people, we just might discover powerful work groups emerging all around the organization. Better yet, we will find ourselves saddled with the wonderful problem of trying to keep up with people who are shining in powerful community-like work groups.

14

Caring, Connecting, and Confirming Scripts

Any change that does not first change the meaning of effective action cannot persist because it continues to expose individuals to potential embarrassment.

from *Knowledge for Action*
... by CHRIS ARGYRIS

Of all the dimensions of organizational life that need to be changed before we can emerge from the shadows and build places to shine, our scripts might be the most sensitive. In the thirty years that I have practiced the art of organizational leadership, I can honestly say that I have had more sleepless nights over unresolved conflict between two or more people than any other single issue. My frustration over not being able to resolve conflict and my concern with the way in which we kill each other's songs without trying were two of the biggest reasons that I went back to school as an adult and completed my master's degree in Organizational Communication, and were also strong driving forces behind this book.

Creating an environment where people not only get along, but actually care for each other, confirm each other, support and encourage each other, seems like an impossible dream at times. That the bookshelves of managers' offices and company libraries are full of tried-and-failed programs proves it. Why is it so hard for us to change our scripts—to stop putting each other down, killing each other's songs, and playing silly "gotcha" games of one-upping each other? In the words of a frustrated manager whom I know, "If I knew the answer to that question I could make a million, retire, and never worry about another people issue as long as I lived." If there are answers, unfortunately they are not easy ones. In order to get at them, we might have to take a journey that we do not wish to take. Because this is such a delicate, yet all-pervasive issue, I am going to go back to the roots and review some of the theories of why we insist on pointing fingers at each other and putting each other down.

Theories about why we put each other down have emerged from several fields. From a biological perspective, we are inclined to blame our genetically programmed drive to ensure our survival and compete for scarce resources. To add to that perspective, anthropologists and psychologists point to our need for power and significance in the face of our own mortality. Other experts suggest that instinctual drives and the psychological battle between the id, the ego, and the superego are at fault. Some point to the modern-day obsession with the self and our need to protect it from embarrassment at all costs. Sociologists and phenomenologists tell us that we merely get into bad habits that become rituals and systems with lives of their own. They remind us that if as members of a group we wish to resolve conflict, we must do more than change the person or persons that are the apparent cause; we must think in terms of behavior systems and change the habits and rituals of the entire group. Each perspective provides insight into the issue. But at the end of the day, the challenge still remains: How do we learn to stop pointing fingers and putting each other down and instead start helping each other shine?

Under the terms of the new social contract at work, the issue of interpersonal scripts will likely grow in importance. Although they differ in their approaches and predictions of what the organizational structures of the future will look like, almost every expert on organizational change agrees on one point: more teams and cross-functional networking will be the order of the day, both within the organization and also between it, other organizations, and the community—and not just the local community, but the global community as well. In the team-based structures of the new organization, learning how to work together and get along with more people will be a prerequisite.

Not long ago, I heard a story about a division that struggled with unhealthy scripts, which might help us get our arms around this issue. Like many other work groups, they were caught in a vicious cycle of put-downs.

On the surface, the problem appeared to rest with the sales manager and the production manager. Most of the members of the group were convinced that if "those two could learn to get along" the problem would be resolved. So the general manager did what all good general managers would have done, faced with the same situation. After trying every method she could think of, including incentives based on teamwork, and still noticing little or no improvement, she sent the offenders to a seminar on interpersonal communications.

To the general manager's dismay, the production manager and the sales manager returned from the seminar as angry at each other as they were before they left. Only now they were both enlightened. Each knew why the conflict existed. It was because the other was interpersonally incompetent. The seminar had only proved their assumptions: it was the other person's fault all along.

The general manager was both disappointed and frustrated. What was she to do next? She decided to send each one away separately to a more intense one-on-one program offered by a reputable local consulting firm staffed with qualified industrial psychologists.

At first the general manager was impressed and pleased with the results of the one-on-one program. The sales manager and the production manager seemed to get along better. She began to brag about the program to other managers she knew. Then one day it all broke loose again. It happened at a staff meeting. The group was talking about a customer who had received his shipment two days late. The leader of the production team claimed that the sales team had given them a wrong date. In the middle of the discussion, one of the members of the sales team announced, "If it weren't for the constant bickering between those two (pointing toward the sales manager and the production manager) this would never have happened; they just don't communicate." To make a long and messy story short, the production manager blew up at the member of the sales team, whereupon the sales manager blew up at the production manager, and the feud was back with all of its previous fury and more.

Here is another story that might sound familiar. It is a story about a small manufacturing company that decided to embark on a quality program and implement a new, team-based structure. The story is made up and the characters are not real, but the events are true to life. I have both observed and participated in groups with similar experiences.

One day, Acme Manufacturing woke up to the knowledge that all their competitors were into the "quality movement." They felt out of place without a quality program of their own and so they decided to implement one, with teams and all. After a quick two-day seminar on teams and team-building, they assigned people to process-improvement teams. The story I will tell is about a team that was assigned the task of writing a new mission for the company, incorporating the principles of quality.

The team consisted of the following members: Jim, the production supervisor; Julie, the marketing manager; Al, the Human Resources manager; and three members of their respective staffs, who will remain unnamed.

Jim was a strong, decisive manager known for his ability to make things happen. He started working for Acme right out of high school. His ability to take charge, make decisions quickly even under pressure, and lead a tough project to its completion was recognized early on in his career. Everyone respected Jim for his strength and decisiveness. Jim was willing to work on the new team if that's what the owner wanted, but deep down he felt that he had better things to do.

Julie had always excelled. It started in grade school with As and starring roles in school activities and culminated with the honor of being valedictorian of her high school graduating class. She started with Acme after graduating from college with honors. Her expert skills in marketing and her ability to learn quickly resulted in a promotion to marketing manager while she was still in her twenties. She knew how to assess a situation and arrive at a recommendation quickly, and she balanced her ability with good interpersonal skills. She felt a bit stifled in her role and welcomed the opportunity to learn from the team experience.

Al loved people. He had loved to work with others for as long as he could remember. Human Resources was a good fit for him. Except for the administrative part, which he often complained that there was way too much of, his skills and interests were well-matched to his job. He looked forward to the team experience with enthusiasm.

The first meeting of the group was a bit clumsy. The people knew each other, but they had never worked together as a team prior to this experience. Thus, they went through the normal feeling-out process that all groups go through as the members tried to determine where they might fit and what would be expected of them. Al had been instructed by the owner to explain their assignment and he did so at the first meeting. Jim listened with a sober look on his face, while Julie took copious notes. The other members of the team threw in a thought now and then, but for the most part they took a wait-and-see posture. Toward the end of the meeting Jim commented that he had a heavy schedule and hoped that the group would "get down to business soon."

The second meeting was much livelier than the first. Jim announced early on that he had been thinking about their assignment and, in fact, had taken the time to draft a charter for the group to review. He hoped the group wouldn't think it was too presumptuous of him, but in the interest of time and busy schedules, he felt they would appreciate his efforts. Upon finishing his brief explanation, he handed each member of the group a copy and sat back in his chair, waiting for their approval.

Al was the first to respond. He thanked Jim for his efforts but suggested that the team needed to work on their charter together. He reminded everyone that they hadn't even decided how they would operate as a team, like the seminar said they should do. He suggested that the team consider Jim's draft later, at a more appropriate time. Julie agreed with Al, as did the two members of the group from their departments. Jim was obviously irritated. He commented that, "If Al knew so much about teams, perhaps he could teach them all," and smiled one of those "in the know" smiles at the other members of the group. Everyone except his own staff member, who smiled sort of off to the side so that not everyone could see him, ignored his efforts to disrupt the process.

For the remainder of the second meeting, Al attempted to lead the group through a process of deciding rules for operating as a team. Jim sat with his arms folded, rolling his eyes and sending other nonverbal signals of frustration to his staff member every now and then.

After the second meeting things went from bad to worse. Jim continued to look bored at every meeting. Now and then he would comment on how the group was going nowhere. Al continued to try to lead a team process. The other members of the group started showing up late or not at all. Julie eventually took charge and led a rather short, but semi-productive meeting or two that resulted in a charter in time to meet the deadline set by the owner. Everyone was glad to see the project come to a close. The words of the frustrated staff member from Julie's group summed it up well: "If that's what teams are all about, leave me out."

I shared these stories not to provide examples of "do's and don't's" for groups and teams. Nor is it my intent to point fingers at certain types of behavior. If there are lessons here at all, I might refer to the first story as an example that conflict is usually bigger than just two people who can't seem to get along, and in fact involves the entire group. From the second story, I might draw the lesson that teams must learn about group tensions and role emergence, particularly the struggle for the role of leader, so that they can find ways to ensure that everyone discovers a meaningful role. Or I could emphasize the importance of dealing with conflict early in the life of a team, in the spirit of open dialogue and on the basis of achieving a gain-gain outcome. Indeed, these are valuable lessons to be learned, but my intent here is not to be analytical or critical, or to offer advice for that matter. I will offer advice later perhaps, but for now I wish to show that human conflict emerges in everyday life as a result of, as Argyris put it, "humans paying strict attention to (being) human"—including practicing their "defensive actions learned through acculturation" (Argyris, 1993).

But we should not let ourselves off the hook so easily. When as leaders we are "just being human," we often kill someone's song without knowing it. For example, the real victims in the two stories I related here are not the feuding production manager and sales manager or even the frustrated general manager of the first story, or Jim, Julie, and Al of the second story, though no doubt life was not pleasant for any of these characters. But the real victims of these unhealthy scripts are the unnamed members of the group, like the member of Jim's staff who was intimidated into following his lead or the member of Julie's staff who struggled through a team experience that left a bitter taste in her mouth for teams in general. In short, our defensive scripts kill our own songs, but more importantly they kill the songs of those around us who may be in a position of lesser power and feel helpless to do anything about it. The rantings and ravings of famous people like Green Bay Packer Coach Vince Lombardi and Chicago Mayor Daley make entertaining conversation at a cocktail party, but for those who were the brunt of their attacks these episodes were not fun in the least. And let us never forget the reality of powerful rulers who live off the energy of others or the intimidation rituals identified by Rory O'Day that I reviewed in Chapter 8.

e that we have on the self-esteem of others, es-
are in the role of leader, is an important one and
...ush it off lightly. Those who study communication point out that we each present ourselves daily and that we
seek the confirmation of others, feedback that says we count—we
are who we think we are. In our culture the most important place
to be confirmed is at work. In the words of Warren Bennis, the
well-known author of several books on leadership, "Work really
defines who we are" (Bennis, 1994).

As we learned earlier, when we present ourselves, whether
at work or at home, three responses can occur. One, we can feel
confirmed, made to believe that we are who we think we are, that
our presence is accepted and respected even if others do not to-
tally agree with our opinions. Two, we can feel *rejected*, made to
believe that our presentation isn't right yet or that our opinion is
uninformed, but still recognized as a person of value nonetheless
and given a chance to prove ourselves. Three, we can feel *disconfirmed*, ignored or treated as if we are someone whose opinion
doesn't count at all, like a child. The third response can be devastating to our self-esteem.

Thomas Kuhn, who completed much of his research on this
issue inside big organizations of the industrial era, coined a term,
orientational other, to describe the effect leaders have on the self-
esteem of their subordinates (Kuhn, 1964). Perhaps he was only
re-discovering what psychoanalysts like Freud had already labeled the *transference phenomenon* that occurs when a patient iden-
tifies the analyst or therapist as a parent figure. Maybe the leaders
of the industrial era were really father figures, or in some cases,
mother figures. Nonetheless, his discoveries are important because
they emphasize the impact that we can have on the self-esteem of
others—especially as leaders. He noted that people most often
looked to their boss for approval when they presented themselves
at work. He also noted that people were often crushed when they
did not receive that approval—and it was happening far more often
than one might think. Experience tells me that although Kuhn's
research was conducted almost forty years ago, the results are still

relevant. People still look toward orientational others for approval and self-confirmation. And often that person is still the boss.

Perhaps these thoughts on the causes and impacts of unhealthy scripts belong back in Chapter 8, but I have included them here for a reason. If as leaders we have the power to disconfirm others and kill their songs, it follows that we also have the power to confirm others and to bring out the song in those who choose to work with us and to follow our lead, not in a way that manipulates people and encourages them to become dependent *resources*, but in a way that confirms their potential as *sources* of energy and light, people who are capable of shining on their own. One way to do that is to do far less *to, for,* and *about* "my people" and much more *with* others who are equal.

Our inability to deal with the issue of unhealthy scripts at work has not escaped the attention of the experts of our day. Peter Senge reminds us that we each carry around a mental model of the way the world should work that influences our daily scripts (Senge, 1994). Harvard professor Chris Argyris, quoted earlier in this chapter, has been writing about scripts in the workplace for a long time. He cites defensive personal behaviors that link to unhealthy rituals as a major roadblock to change in the organization (Argyris, 1993). William Glasser writes about a theory of human behavior based on picture albums in our heads. In these albums are pictures for meeting our basic needs for survival, belonging, freedom, power, and fun, complete with scripts for meeting each one of these needs (Glasser, 1984). He reveals that we continue to practice these scripts long after they have lost their effectiveness. For example, we might choose to depress in order to meet our need for belonging even though our behavior frustrates and alienates the people we love. Erving Goffman, who probably wrote more than any single sociologist about scripts and interaction rituals, points out that we are all experts at presenting and protecting the self in our everyday scripts, whether we choose to acknowledge it or not. He asserts that this thing we call the self is a social construct with a life of its own and that we will go to great pains to keep it alive. The point is that experts from several fields have raised the issue of unhealthy scripts and identified them as barriers to healthy interaction in the workplace.

How, then, do we learn to practice new, healthier scripts? Here too the advice is plentiful. Senge suggests that we learn to deal with creative tension (the difference between what we have and what we want) by searching for the truth in open dialogue. Argyris argues for a more scientific approach, involving diagnosis through mapping our behavior, seeing the error of our ways, articulating new models of behavior, and the use of ongoing intervention by a qualified facilitator to keep us on track and bring us back when our behavior falls short of matching our new model. Both Senge and Argyris argue for a more systems-thinking approach that encourages us to see the vicious cycles of our own scripts and rituals. Glasser argues for changing our scripts, and says that we indeed have more power over what we do than the pop behaviorists have led us to believe. He points out that a behavior consists of four parts: thinking, feeling, doing, and physiological responses, like sweating when we are nervous. Although we might not be able to easily change the way we think and feel, we can always change what we do. And guess what? Since all four dimensions of our behavior are connected, when we change what we do, our thoughts, feelings, and physiological responses will naturally follow. Still others attack this issue from the perspective of developing interpersonal competence through learning new skills. The shelves of bookstores and managers' offices alike are full of books that offer formulas for dealing with human conflict and a set of new skills for getting along at work.

Unfortunately for us, changing unhealthy scripts isn't that easy. If it were, we wouldn't have so many consultants running around showing us how to resolve, or at least manage, conflict. In the introduction to the paperback edition of his book, Peter Senge shares what he has learned about implementing learning strategies and his frustration over this issue. He writes, "There seems to be a particular lack of appetite in many American corporations for the hard work of articulating our mental models conceptually" (Senge, 1994). Argyris admits to similar frustrations after working several years with a consulting firm (Argyris, 1993).

My master's degree is in Organizational Communication and I can honestly say that I have personally tried several approaches based on systems thinking, skill development, conflict management, cultural change, and other hybrid approaches to get at this issue. Although I have experienced positive results, I have also discovered that the issue needs more than a surface fix-it approach if we are going to emerge from the shadows of our put-down scripts at work and build places to shine. Like most issues, we need to address this one with our hearts as well as our heads.

Two people have influenced my thinking on this issue more than any others. One of them is the psychologist Carl Rogers, who created the concept of client-centered therapy. He taught me the meaning of unconditional acceptance and the real power of connecting to people without judging them or expecting them to behave in ways I thought were best for them. He restored my faith in the potential of the human spirit and revealed to me how powerful it can be when people are allowed to connect to their work and each other. The second person who has influenced my thinking on this issue is the philosopher Martin Buber, whom I have quoted throughout this book. He added to Rogers' thinking an emphasis on believing in the human potential of each person. His concept of "making present" is a powerful way to look at human interaction. Buber went so far as to assert that human relationships are the source of personal growth. I will quote him here. Though his use of the masculine is dated, his message is still profound.

> The inmost growth of the self is not induced by man's relation to himself, "as people like to suppose today", but by the confirmation in which one man knows himself to be "made present" in his uniqueness by the other. "Self-reflection" that vague shibboleth which occupies so large a place in our popular culture, is not the goal but the by-product. The goal is completing distance by relation, and relation here means mutual confirmation, co-operation, and genuine dialogue.

Human conflict is a fact of life. Regardless of how much we learn about this issue or how many new interpersonal skills master, we will continue to put each other down even though we may not intend to, if for no other reason than that we feel the need to protect ourselves from embarrassment or fear of being put down ourselves. However, if we are going to have a chance to emerge from the shadows of our unhealthy scripts at work and begin to build places to shine, we need to tap into the power of relationships. This means that we need to dare to be present for each other, to look at each other as valuable pieces of art in whose presence we should stand in awe, or as unfolding novels whose last and best chapter is yet to be written, in full awareness that we will hurt each other now and then and be forced to ask for forgiveness. A view of people any less powerful than this will encourage us to continue to put each other down and kill each other's songs without regard for the consequences of our behaviors.

I realize that I have not answered all of the questions about unhealthy scripts. Nor have I provided a perfect plan for writing new, healthier scripts. In truth, I do not believe that I or anyone else can come up with such a plan. The human species is too wonderfully complicated for that. But in all fairness, I can provide some practical advice in the form of what I call *rays of light* to get us started building relationships that encourage shining in the workplace. If nothing else, these rays of light can show us a path out from the shadows of our own scripts and lead us to a place to shine. One of these rays of light I have already introduced: unconditional acceptance. The other two are: 2) a willingness to let go, and 3) a readiness to try on new scripts.

Since I have already introduced the idea of unconditional acceptance, I will keep my comments brief. However, I would point out that unconditional acceptance has two parts. The first is to learn to love, accept, and trust yourself. The second is to do the same with others. I am not certain which comes first, accepting yourself or others, but I do know that they go together. We cannot love and accept others if we do not love and accept ourselves. This is a difficult issue to deal with, but I have learned an amazingly simple truth: the most effective way for me to learn to understand myself is to understand others.

The second ray of light that I offer to help show the way to healthier scripts at work is to learn to let go. It sounds simple. It is and it isn't. On one hand, we are granted permission to release ourselves of the responsibility to control and fix everything, including ourselves and others. On the other hand, we are asked to lose control of our very selves and to trust in the forces of the human spirit, yet to remain responsible in our efforts to encourage open dialogue and to bring harmony to human interaction. It is a balancing act that will come up again in Chapter 18, but for now I wish to point out that in order to write new, healthier scripts we will need to let go of the old ones. In offering his own advice on how to change unhealthy behaviors in the organization, Charles Handy borrows a phrase from Keats who wrote it way back in 1817: *a negative capability*. Keats defined this critical capability as follows: "when a man is capable of being in uncertainties, mysteries, and doubts" (Handy, 1990). Letting go is hard. It requires a willingness to forgive ourselves and others and to live with uncertainty for awhile. It helps if we dare to be present for each other and to share our uncertainty. Indeed, sharing our fears builds the kind of trust that is needed to hold scripts together when the going gets rough—as long as we are careful not to force people to share what they are not ready to share.

The third ray of light that I will offer is a readiness to try on new scripts. This too is hard to do. But it is made much easier by the rays of light cast by unconditional acceptance of oneself and others and the willingness to let go of old scripts. Nonetheless, it requires courage to take the first step. I have discovered that the kind of courage needed to try on new scripts is found in relationships. In other words, it helps to do it with others who care. But then, scripts always take more than one person to complete. Therefore, bringing others into the act at some point should be natural. It also helps to play at new scripts and to have fun doing it. Remember, humans learn through play. But if you can't find someone who wants to play with you, try on new scripts anyway. Start treating people as if they are pieces of art, or players in a script with special stories of their own whose best chapters are yet to be written. You will be amazed at the results.

I will close this chapter with a story and a little vignette. The story is about someone I know who has defined the meaning of unconditional acceptance with his own life; the vignette is about the lost art of play.

George

I met George years ago. Even then I knew there was something special about him. Like others who knew him, I took him for granted. It was an easy thing to do because he was always willing to listen. He was just there for you.

George was a professor at a major university. You would never have guessed it from his demeanor. He expressed with his presence a kind of humility that emerged from a genuine love for himself and others. Indeed, the most special thing about George was his presence. He was always and in all ways present for people. I recall thinking over the years how unusual and wonderful it was for a university professor to be so available to others—even students. Frankly, most of the professors I had known were too busy with their research, writing a book, or complaining of a heavy student load. But George was never preoccupied with such things. He was always there for people.

Years after I met George I began to realize the extent of his influence. Everywhere I went I ran into people who would tell me stories about how he had been present for them. I also learned that he suffered from a chronic illness. But one would never have known, because George never talked much about himself.

Over the years, I have run into a few Georges—even inside big organizations. They are rare, but they are around, nonetheless. Often one must look in the less obvious places to find them. They aren't into status and titles, though some of them are leaders in the organization. You know who they are by their willingness to accept you and others unconditionally and to listen with their hearts.

We need more Georges in our world—people who are willing to be present for others and accept them unconditionally for who they are becoming. More importantly, we need more Georges in leadership roles in our organizations. They bring light into the shadows at work and inspire us to believe in ourselves and each other.

A Tiger in the Alfalfa Patch

I will be a lion
And you shall be a bear
And each of us will have a den
Beneath the nursery chair
And you must growl and growl and growl,
And I will roar and roar,
And then—why then—you'll growl again
And I will roar some more!

from *Wild Beasts*
. . . by EVALEEN STEIN

As I child I played a game with my brothers and sisters—all nine of them—called "jungle animal." All that was needed in order to play was an alfalfa patch and a child's imagination. Or you could try a tiger lily patch. But even make-believe lions and tigers make tracks. And if your mom and dad were anything like mine, they didn't appreciate trails through the lilies. On the other hand, alfalfa fields were large enough to absorb several small knee prints without showing much damage.

We would play jungle animal for hours. My favorite animal was a tiger. My sister Sandra preferred a lion. We would slither and stalk our way through the alfalfa patch as if it were a real jungle with real jungle plants and real jungle animals around every corner. After awhile we could even hear the mimicking of the jungle parrots and the sound of crickets or the wind rustling through the thick undergrowth. Playing jungle was so much fun that we often ignored Mom's call for dinner. After all, who can hear a voice through the sounds of the jungle?

As the years passed I outgrew the game of jungle animal. I am not sure why. Perhaps I grew too tall for the alfalfa stems, or maybe it was the disapproving looks, the mocking laughter, or being made fun of by the bigger boys who thought it was silly to play jungle. Whatever the reason, playing jungle was tucked away in my memory and seldom came out to bother my consciousness again.

Then one day I was told that I had cancer. I was forced to take time off from my busy schedule. I took long walks in the country. On one of these walks I noticed an alfalfa patch in full bloom. Suddenly, the memory of playing jungle animal was as clear as the day I tucked it away. I saw my brothers and sisters crawling through the alfalfa stems with me, the tiger, stalking at their heels. I remembered how much fun it was to play jungle animal. And I wondered why I ever quit playing.

I can't help believing that if we let our guard down more often, let our child-like imaginations run a little wild, and dared to lose ourselves in the art of play, we would enjoy our work and each other more and even get more done in the process. As an added benefit, we would tap into a source of energy that seems to be missing from many work environments and one that is sorely needed in these times of rapid change. Anthropologist Edward Hall reminds us that play is a necessary part of learning new skills and ways of relating to our work and each other. In fact, it is an important part of the development process of all mammals (Hall, 1976). All we need to do to appreciate the role of play is to watch primates learn or small children play at being adults. It is through play that we learn new things and adapt to change. Furthermore, play has its own rewards. It is rewarding just to engage in it and it produces energy—it helps us shine.

Ken Gergen takes the notion of play as a way to facilitate healthy change into the workplace. He writes about *serious play*—a spirited way of deeply but safely exploring patterns that have significant longer-term implications (Gergen, 1984). I doubt that we need the experts to tell us something we already know in our hearts. Work and play are often one and the same. In fact, when work loses its playful nature, it deteriorates into "being worked" or merely "a job."

If you find it difficult to play at work, reflect on a childhood game. Think of a time when you were having so much fun that you forgot yourself in the sheer joy of it. And if you still can't come up with a picture of what it is like to play, call a friend or give me a call. But don't be surprised if I am not there to answer the phone. Most likely I am busy playing tiger in the alfalfa patch.

15

Where Do We Go from Here?

Miracles happen after a lot of hard work.
from *Plain and Simple*
. . . by SUE BENDER

I realize that by asking people to build places to shine where
they work, I am asking them to break new ground, to go against
much of what they have been taught in school as well as by the
organizations where they work. In truth, I am asking people to
change the way they feel, think, structure, and act in relation to
their work, each other, and the organization itself. What makes
this kind of change even more difficult is that it is hard to measure in a left-brain world. I also recognize that unless I can bring
these concepts down to a level where they actually affect our daily
lives, they will remain merely concepts, good ideas that have little value in real life.

One of my challenges early on in working with groups in all
kinds of different work environments was to find a way to make
a place to shine operational, to take it beyond the abstract dimensions of feeling and thinking and to actually effect a change

... ~~~~~~~—and then to be able to take what I had learned and offer it in the form of practical advice in this book, a way for people to see the light and change their ways.

How will we come to see the light? Based on working with and observing several groups in the organization, my own divisions included, and my research in small groups in the classroom, I have discovered that it helps to have a common language, especially one that touches a deep place in our hearts where we all long for more meaning and purpose in life. I have discovered that "a place to shine" does that. It also helps to have a way to frame the concepts that are part of a place to shine. It makes it easier to discover the shadows and embrace them for what they are and to envision new ways to relate to our work and each other. For this, the model of theories, structures, and scripts seemed to work effectively. But a language and a model were not enough. Something was still missing.

Some experts on social transformation say that during times of rapid change a creative process is at work, propelling the change. It is a natural and spontaneous process that is often hidden from the view of those who are part of the change. One of the most successful transformations in modern times has been what is commonly referred to as the South African miracle. Kobus Neethling, a transformation consultant in Waterloof, South Africa, suggests that the reason that the transformation in South Africa has evolved with a minimum of violence and bloodshed is that people began to acknowledge the process at work and learned to help it move in a healthy direction. The phases of the process that he describes are consistent with the steps of creative thinking and problem-solving found in other models, but the number and exact descriptions of the phases are not the important points here. The important point is that a natural process unfolded and that it was helped along in a way that led to a healthier place. This was a part of the puzzle that was missing in my earlier thinking.

The importance of recognizing an underlying process at work is that it helps one understand why things are moving in a certain direction and how one can influence the process, help it along, so to speak, and move it in a positive direction. Mihaly

Csikszentmihalyi reminds us that the flow of evolution has always been a tug-of-war between two forces: on one hand are the natural forces of entropy that cause things to fall apart. On a personal level, entropy is manifested in the form of regrets, blaming, jealousy, and other forms of violence that we enact toward ourselves and our world. On an organizational level, entropy sets in when we allow the system to take over and define our work for us, or when we stick our heads in the clouds and ignore the cry for meaning in our work and our relationships. Fighting against the forces of entropy are the forces of harmony. They are manifested in learning, loving, working, and playing at new forms, and building relationships to our work, each other, and purposes that transcend the immediate. Species that tap into the forces of harmony and cooperate with and influence the processes of evolution in a positive direction are the ones that will survive into the next millennium and beyond. Csikszentmihalyi asserts that this will require both *differentiation*, developing our special gifts, and *integration*, a capacity to connect to others and to weave our gifts into a life theme with purposes that transcend the immediate gratification of our desires and the organizational imperatives of profits and growth (Csikszentmihalyi, 1993).

One can choose to ignore the natural processes of change, or worse yet, to fight them, but they will not go away. The ancient wisdom of the Tao reminds us that if we ignore or fight against the natural processes of life, they may take a course that we do not like. They may move toward entropy and violence—or the process itself may grow from our negative energy to take over and control us. Letting the process of change control us is much like giving our work over to the organization so that it can define our work for us. In the end, we may not like how it gets defined. On the other hand, if we acknowledge the process and work in cooperation with it, we can steer it in a positive direction. What's more, we can experience the power of the process to connect people in a common cause and to provide them with an opportunity to discover a meaningful role. It is a wonderful opportunity to confirm each other and to form a bond around a common vision.

A transformation is taking place at work. It is more subtle and far less violent, at least on the surface, than the transformation of a nation, but it has some of the same characteristics. One of these characteristics is an underlying process. The whole point of this book is that we have the opportunity and the responsibility to influence this process in ways that bring light into the workplace and help people emerge from the shadows at work and build places to shine, "places where each individual is confirmed as a special person capable of making a unique and significant contribution to the whole in the presence of others who care." In order to do that, perhaps we need to understand the underlying process better, the subject of the next chapter.

16

A Source of Light:

The Power of Connecting

Why does prosperity drive us apart?
And adversity bring us together?

. . . G. FROST

If there is a process for change already taking place, how do we influence that process in ways that promote the kind of harmony that respects the individual, yet taps into the power of connecting our work to each other and purposes that transcend the immediate? One way is to learn more about the process itself, especially to learn from those who are already in the process of building places to shine. They offer a source of light that can help us on our own journeys. I am going to share a process model based on the work of experts in the transformation of cultures, like Kobus Neethling, mentioned in the previous chapter, plus my own work with departments and divisions I have managed over the years and groups of people I have worked with in academia as well as other organizations.

Before I share a model for the process of transforming a place to work into a place to shine, I must qualify it. First, I must remind you, again, that this is not a process that one creates or forces; rather, it is a spontaneous process that occurs with or without us. The second qualifier may seem like a contradiction to the first, but it is really one of those complementary paradoxes of change. It is this. Although we must accept the underlying process and not fight it, we can influence the process in ways that help it along and move it on a healthier course. Moreover, we can tap into the energy of people working together to bring about a better world. In this regard, there are lessons to be learned from those who have influenced transformations in ways that minimized violence and produced healthier outcomes, such as the South African miracle. Some of the examples of groups in the workplace who are building places to shine that I shared earlier may bring this lesson closer to home.

The third qualifier is that this process is not intended to be a fixed, linear model for transforming the workplace. For one thing, it is more circular, not linear, as you will discover; for another, it is only one way to frame the process; thus I could be missing a phase or two, or I might have included one too many. Furthermore, the process might not be a process at all. It might be a series of hurdles to cross or critical events that must be lived through before change becomes part of a new way of life. The power of the model lies not in its perfection, rather in its ability to provide a metaphor for the journey, a map to follow, a way to connect people around a common vision and to help them learn new, healthier scripts as they interact in the process and learn the joy of building new, healthier places to work together. Its real power might lie in its ability to tap into a source of light that is needed in order to build places to shine: the power of connecting.

Finally, I must point out that even though I have attempted to define the clouds that can get in the way of the process during each phase, in reality they are spread throughout the process. When and where these clouds emerge depends on the group and the work environment. With these caveats, I will list six possible phases or events of the transformation process. I hope they will help us to see what is going on in the American workplace in general, and to identify where your organization or work group fits into the process. In each phase I will include a brief description of the clouds to watch out for, along with some suggestions on how we might influence the process in ways that minimize the negative effects of these clouds and keep us moving on our journey to a place to shine.

PHASE ONE: RECOGNIZING THE MESS AND EMBRACING THE SHADOWS

The first step in the process of transformation is the recognition that things just are not working the way they should be. But usually it needs to go beyond a mere recognition that things could be better. In fact, often it takes a crisis in the form of an event or a series of events to bring this home. At the level of a country, often a violent act serves as the catalyst for recognizing that people are in a mess, such as the Soweto uprising of 1976 in South Africa.

On a personal level, a crisis can force recognition of a messed-up life. I am reminded of the alcoholic who acknowledges that he is indeed an alcoholic and needs help. Often he recognizes this only after reaching bottom or experiencing the feelings of total despair. In the words of a friend, "I was sick and tired of being sick and tired." A health issue or a confrontation with one's mortality can be a catalyst for change. In my own case, cancer changed my life. In any event, it often takes a crisis to recognize the mess we are in.

In the workplaces of America, people are beginning to recognize that we are in a mess. As I pointed out in Chapter 10, people are beginning to talk and write about the need for new connections and a change of heart. At first, change was driven by the recognition that we are not competitive in world markets. Panic set in as organizations struggled to introduce quality, maintain continuous improvement, and "reengineer" themselves. Downsizing was one of the violent offshoots of this panic. Now, we are beginning to look deeper into the shadows at work, at our theories, structures, and scripts. And we are discovering that the mess is worse than we thought. We have damaged the relationship between us and ourselves, our work, and each other. People aren't shining at work because they aren't feeling connected or appreciated. We have also discovered that we must do more than improve our processes and reengineer our organizations. We must transform them into places where people can connect to their work and each other in more meaningful ways.

Experience tells us that we only move beyond the messes we are in when we embrace the shadows, forgive ourselves and each other, tap into the energy within and between us, and move on. This lesson applies to the workplace as well. Work groups I know that have moved to a place to shine, my own included, have learned this lesson—often the hard way, by facing conflict that cannot be resolved using our normal approach based on sheer willpower or a new set of skills. Working with a division that learned to care, I believe that we gained more from facing the truth of our own shadows than we did from all the quick-fix programs put together.

Some companies are discovering this truth. I am told that Southwest Airlines is one. In spite of operating in a highly competitive environment where many companies have failed, they are doing well because they have embraced the shadows of the old system and are in the process of building a place to shine. I have read about others as well. In the process they are learning to care for the only asset that makes any difference, long-term: people.

On a personal note, one of the most valuable insights I am gaining from my encounter with cancer is the knowledge that the shadows are friendly and much is to be learned from getting to know them better. Cancer has forced me to take the time to reflect on my own life and to make peace with, even learn to love, the parts of myself that I was running away from. I have learned to embrace the shadows and realized in doing so a new freedom to love and to work. I now know that embracing the shadows is a hurdle one must cross before one can become whole and experience the richness of a life of giving freely from one's true self. In the famous words of the great philosopher Albert Camus, "In the depth of winter, I finally learned that within me lay an invincible summer." There is a lesson here that goes beyond my personal awakening and applies to the process of building a place to shine at work.

Several years ago I presented parts of my early vision of a place to shine to a group of managers in an information system division of a major company. I warned the group that building a place to shine would require an honest and open look at the shadows in the system itself. I told them that as leaders they would likely be challenged to give up power as the concept is typically defined and discover the power of being vulnerable and caring. I suggested that as a group they might experience chaos for a while. A wise woman in the back of the room raised her hand. "There're no shortcuts to heaven," she said.

The wisdom of this woman's words sunk in slowly. I didn't realize how profound they were until I began to work with my own division and other groups in their efforts to build places to shine. I then discovered the hard way that the woman had been right. There are no shortcuts to a better place. It takes a willingness to embrace the shadows.

In his book, *The Different Drum: Community Making and Peace*, M. Scott Peck writes about the process of building community. He cites four steps: 1) pseudocommunity, 2) chaos, 3) emptiness, and 4) community (Peck, 1987). Not unlike the models that have emerged from studies of small groups, such as the popular forming, storming, norming, performing model based on the research of Bruce Tuckman or the work of Ernest Bormann at the University of Minnesota on symbolic conversion, research shows that in order for a bunch of people to become a cohesive work group, they must be willing to go through the valley of the shadows of their own humanness (Bormann, 1990). Bormann says that becoming a community-like, cohesive work group is like peeling an onion—tears and all. What a wonderful and poignant analogy! Based on my own experiences and research, this analogy applies in the workplace. In order to build a place where people shine, the shadows of the organization must be acknowledged and embraced—tears and all.

Talking about an organization as a community introduces an oxymoron in many ways. Can there be such a thing as an organized community when, in truth, an organization must be willing to be unorganized, at least for a while, if it wishes to become a place to shine? Margaret Wheatley addresses this question and suggests that only organizations that are willing to discover order in chaos have a shot at building community-like cultures where people shine. Peck's model would tend to tell us that chaos is a necessary step in the process of becoming a community. Thus, to say that organizations are communities can be a contradiction unless the organization is willing to face its own shadows and learn from them.

The message that organizations must be willing to embrace the shadows built into their theories, structures, and scripts is a hard one for leaders in the organization to swallow. In essence, the message says that organizations must become *un*organized in order to become places to shine. It is like asking something to be what it exists not to be. If organizations exist to control things and deny chaos, then asking leaders to risk losing control and trusting that order will emerge from relationships between people and their work and other people whom they serve (customers) and work with is like asking them to give up their source of security—indeed their very sense of identity. However, we will not transform places to work into places to shine unless we are willing to embrace the shadows, in essence, to acknowledge the mess we are in.

Clouds to Watch Out For in Phase One

As promised, I am going to describe clouds that can get in the way of the transformation process within each phase. In phase one, the most common cloud is the *cloud of minimization*. I was tempted to name it the cloud of denial, but I think minimization gets closer to the truth. It isn't that we deny that the problem exists. Rather, the clouds of minimization lure us into thinking that the problem is not as serious as it seems. "Just hang in there and things will get better," or "The organization will fix things if you give it time and let it," or "People need to grow up and take charge of their own lives," are common phrases that line the clouds of minimization. I cannot record the number of times I have been told by groups that the shadows at work are not as dark as I paint them, or that things are getting better, or that it is not their responsibility to change things. No doubt things are getting better in some places, but the shadows at work still loom large and thick in many places and minimizing them will not make them go away.

Another set of clouds that can rear their ugly heads in step one of the process are the *clouds of blame*. These clouds encourage us to look for scapegoats, someone or something to blame. This clouded thinking can lead us into conflict that produces more shadows to deal with than when we started. Later, in phase three, when I write about gathering the facts, I will point out the importance of dealing with the issue as opposed to the people. For now it is enough to warn you that merely blaming someone or something for the shadows at work will cause the process to move in a negative direction; you need to move beyond blaming to embracing the shadows and dealing with issues.

A third set of clouds that can emerge from the first two and become far more dangerous and damaging to the process of healthy change are the *clouds of resistance*. Another name for them is the clouds of panic. In the organization, the best example of these clouds is the massive layoffs of people in an effort to cut costs and become competitive. A statement I heard the other day captures this clouded thinking well: "Fixed costs walk in on two feet and they walk out on two feet." I think this person was trying to tell me that the only way to improve the health of the organization was to cut costs and that the easiest way to do that is to lay off people. Laying off people without involving them in the decision process or looking for healthier alternatives can damage the soul of a company. It can take years to recover and build back trust. It is a clouded way of thinking with a big price tag attached to it. We are just now beginning to pay the price.

PHASE TWO: THE DESIRE TO CHANGE

A desire to change must be present if the process of transformation is to continue in a healthy direction. That sentence might be
the biggest understatement I have made in this entire book.
Without a desire to make things better, the process of transforming a workplace into a place to shine won't go anywhere except perhaps to the coffee table to be batted back and forth with
the rest of the complaints of the day. And it must be a strong
enough desire to motivate action and to continue to do so
throughout the process. This is where the need for leadership en-
ters the scene. Often the passion of a bold leader keeps the desire alive when the clouds of helplessness overwhelm people.
Leaders can also play an important role in blending differing
goals into a common vision.

A truth I have learned about organizations is that they are
not as organized as we might have thought. In reality, organizations represent a mixture of goals and people's desires that come
together now and then in the form of plans and shared goals. They
usually come together in smaller pockets of people, where people blend their personal goals and visions with the common goal
or shared vision of a department or a work group. The hope is
that these group goals connect to company goals and ultimately
to a company vision that can be shared by all the groups in the
company. The same thing must happen with the desire to change.
Several differing desires, some personal, some group-centered,
must come together and form a common blend. Healthy groups
have learned the art of blending desires and goals without destroying them. Experts in group process call it *differentiating* and
integrating. It helps to have a vision, but it must be a vision born
out of a process within the group and owned by the group. It must
also be a vision that respects and welcomes diversity and honors
the individual as well as the group.

In the case of transformation in the workplace I have suggested that the common vision is a place to shine, a place where
the "specialness" of you and everyone else is appreciated and peo-

ple are respected for who they are becoming. How that gets interpreted and made real is up to each individual and group. In fact, if the individual and the group do not take ownership and build their own vision of a place to shine, the desire will dissipate with time and eventually people will go back into the shadows and hide. It is important to note that the blending of diverse desires for change into a vision that everyone can believe in does not destroy the differences; rather it brings them together around a common theme while respecting different perspectives in the spirit of many voices, one song.

One way to create a shared vision is to use the theory, structure, script model. One group I know constructed a before-and-after model showing the old theories, structures, and scripts in the left column and the new ones in the right. Another group drew a wheel with spokes and different dimensions between the spokes that related to each one of the human senses. The point is to get specific. Visions that inspire lay out a clear picture so that people know what a place to shine would look like (structure), what people would think about their work and each other (theories), and how people would act toward each other (scripts), and in general, what it would feel like to work there. If built and owned by everyone, visions can create and sustain the desire for change.

Clouds to Watch Out For in Phase Two

One of the clouds most frequently encountered in phase two is the *cloud of helplessness*. It is manifested in the notion that there is nothing anyone can do that will make a difference. After all, the system is bigger than all of us. It is also known as the *cloud of negativism*. Faced with the odds, it is so easy to give up the struggle.

Mihaly Csikszentmihalyi provides four reasons why negative thinking is so natural for us. For one thing, there is so much that is negative around us. There are so many reasons to give up. Secondly, we are probably genetically programmed to think the worst. It has served a purpose along the path of evolution by warning us of potential danger and preparing us for the worst. The third reason negative thinking is so common is that it is contagious and addictive. Once we get caught in a vicious cycle of negativism it is hard to crawl out of it. Finally, the mass media has learned how to tap into our fears and our inclination to think the worst. Television sets and tabloids bombard us with negative messages. We, in turn, give these messages energy by paying attention to them. Watching "bad news" on TV or reading sensational stories from tabloids just gives us more reasons to be negative. Whatever the cause, the clouds of helplessness and negativism move the process of change in the wrong direction, toward conflict, chaos, and entropy.

Another set of clouds that appear in phase two are the *clouds of conflict avoidance*. If we are not careful to respect different approaches to the same issue, the process can get overshadowed by these clouds. In my own case I have come to accept the fact that others who believe in a place to shine may take a different approach and emphasize personal responsibility or skill development, whereas I may call for a change of heart and a willingness to connect to each other and confirm each other. But that does not mean that they believe in a place where people are encouraged to shine in their work any less than I do. They merely have a different approach. I have discovered that when I mix these different approaches with mine without destroying their value, together we can form a powerful blend.

PHASE THREE: FACT-FINDING AND ROLE-FINDING

The third phase or critical event in the process of transformation I am using here is a gathering of the facts and a forming of roles. This is where the process can become powerful if you let it, for two reasons. First, it is in this phase that people begin to mobilize and form groups and experience the power of a common vision, and more importantly, the power of working together and confirming each other. Secondly, as people gather the facts they begin to see the shadows for what they are, to understand that they were caused by people being people and organizations being organizations. If done right, gathering the facts can break up the clouds of blame. It forces people to look at the issue and not the person.

I have discovered two things groups can do to bring out the power potential of this phase. One is to use the framework of the theory, structure, script model to go on a shadow hunt. The other is to form working groups, what Mihaly Csikszentmihalyi called *cells* and Helgeson called *webs of inclusion*, and to begin to organize in ways that provide for meaningful roles for the individual while increasing the power to influence change by working in groups.

First, use of the theory, structure, script model can be an effective way to get at the shadows in the system. Some groups start with scripts, since that is the more tangible aspect, and move toward structures and then theories. Other groups simply schedule a brainstorming session and start making a list on flip charts. The important thing to remember is that all must be given an opportunity to express their feelings and thoughts openly. Sometimes focus groups using third parties helps. Questionnaires can work, but they lose the power of interaction—especially the interaction with leaders in the organization who need to be visible in this process. The most effective programs are those where management is willing to get involved in the process of open dialogue and embrace the shadows in the system that keep people from shining. Chris Argyris offers an example of this in his book about the intervention work he did with a consulting firm (Argyris, 1993).

The second source of power that can be tapped in this phase comes from forming cells of people who care about shining in the workplace. As mentioned earlier, Csikszentmihalyi uses this concept to show how people can get involved in influencing change (Csikszentmihalyi, 1993). He describes a cell this way: "The ideal unit for accomplishing a task is a group small enough to allow intense face-to-face interaction, one in which members participate voluntarily, and in which each person can contribute to a common goal by doing what he or she knows best" (Csikszentmihalyi,

1993). He goes on to describe the four major tasks that must be attended to in a cell.

First, is the task of acquiring information and resources from the environment. For this task you need someone who can gather the facts about what is right and wrong. In the case of building a place to shine, the task is to discover the shadows in the theories, structures, and scripts of the system. The second task is to coordinate the activities of the cell or group. Here you need someone to synthesize the information about the environment, including the shadows, and to put it into an order that can be dealt with. This requires facilitating open dialogue within the group about the causes of the shadows and how the group might embrace them for what they are and emerge from them. The third task is to mobilize the energy of the group and to focus it on clearly articulated and achievable goals. It involves the task of scheduling meetings and coordinating assignments and activities within the group. The fourth and final task is to develop and maintain values and beliefs that give the group hope, identity, and purpose. The task involves integrating information into the group's reason for being.

The tasks outlined above can be shared in the group or rotated between individuals, but it is important to note that a leader must emerge, someone the group looks to when they need to understand the vision or move forward and address the task. I will speak more about the role of the leader in the next chapter. The message to be absorbed here is that the most effective and powerful way to operate in the fact-finding phase of transformation is to organize in groups. Calling them cells is to use a metaphor that gives them life and encourages people to think in terms of cells connecting to other cells in the system and in other systems. It can be a powerful metaphor. For example, I know of a cell that formed in a division of a large company and discovered that they were writing a new vision for the entire division. It just so happened that the energy in their group spread to other cells and eventually led to recognition by the general manager, who adapted the original cell's vision as the division's vision. Their simple but powerful vision was this: "We will be a place where everyone is made to feel special." Indeed, cells that form in the fact-finding phase can have a profound influence on steering transformation toward a positive end.

Clouds to Watch Out For in Phase Three

The clouds to watch out for in phase three share a common root: *fear*. I will cover these clouds in this phase, but the truth is that they often appear in phase one and they continue to appear throughout the process. I will speak to five of the fears, but there are probably more.

The first fear is *fear of the facts*. Fear of the facts is often based on the personal fear that one will look stupid. Leaders fear looking stupid for having bought into a system that cast shadows with its theories that limited the human potential, its structures that kept people from connecting to their work and each other, and its scripts that encouraged people to control others and to put each other down. Followers fear looking stupid for having followed the lead of those who had power in the system, for letting themselves "get used," as a frustrated member of my audience put it one day.

A wise mentor of mine reminded me once that there is wisdom in the old aphorism: the truth hurts. The reason the truth hurts is that it breaks down the order that is maintained by little white lies and sometimes big ugly ones. The truth is uncontrollable and unpredictable. It opens the door to new ways of thinking, feeling, and acting, but it asks us to lose ourselves for awhile in the process and to trust in the positive power of connecting around purposes and people. Nevertheless, I have discovered that the facts are friendly. They can be a source of light that moves us beyond blaming and helps us deal with the issues.

Fear of losing control is another cloud that often appears in this phase and keeps reappearing along the way. We have all been taught to believe that we can control ourselves and the world around us—especially those of us who succeeded in the system. In fact, one of the loud messages of the industrial era was: learn to control yourself. But the truth is we control far less than we think. We can influence the natural processes around us by our response to them and we can choose our attitude based on our own values, but we cannot control them. Too often it takes a major crisis in our lives, like cancer, to bring this message home. People who learn to accept that they are not in control and to influence the process in their own way by choosing how to shine and connect to others find their way through these clouds and learn to control what they can and to carve out ways to shine even in the shadows.

A third cloud of fear is the *fear of intimacy*. Intimacy requires that one let go and get lost in the unpredictability of relationships. This can be a scary thing to do if one is not used to it. It ties into the fear of losing control. In the organization we call human relationship issues the "soft stuff." But in our hearts we know that this is really the hard stuff. Perhaps that's why we call it the soft stuff— because deep down we are really afraid of relationships. They are unpredictable, full of conflict, and they come complete with claims and responsibilities. We need to be careful with this one and never forget to respect each person's right to share only what he or she is ready to share. In truth, by accepting each other, including our right to share only what we are ready to share with each other, we build the kind of trust that promotes sharing and caring.

As dehumanizing as the shadows at work can be, they can also provide safety and a temporary sense of security. Crawling out from them not only exposes the blemishes that we have been hiding, it also blinds us for awhile. It brings out another set of clouds, the *fear of claims and responsibilities*. Once we let our guard down and begin to connect to people at a deeper level, we expose ourselves to claims and responsibilities. We are asked to live up to our own expectations as well as the expectations of others. We are urged to consider the feelings of others before we act out our scripts. This can be a frightening responsibility—especially if we are not accustomed to it. But those who dare to be intimate discover the joy of confirming others and being confirmed in return, the kind of joy and energy that Martin Buber tried to capture in his concept of *making present*.

The fifth and final cloud I will cover here is the *fear of conflict*. Like the other clouds of fear, conflict is feared because it is chaotic and unpredictable. It exposes all kinds of things we would rather keep hidden. Consequently, when we sense conflict, we reach into our bag of scripts and pull out our best defensive rituals. However, experts warn us that unless we are willing to go into conflict and learn from it, we make it worse. It is not unlike the mistake of ignoring or fighting the process of change itself. One can do it, but at a price. Stifled or forced conflict will become a big storm cloud that leads to song-killing rituals and command control structures—anything we can think up that might contain it and keep it from spreading. In his book about community-building, Scott Peck warns that the natural tendency is to move from chaos to organization (Peck, 1987). But it is a serious mistake. The only road to true community is through conflict. We learn and grow through embracing conflict. And the joy of embracing differences and learning from conflict is a joy that can be powerful. It is a feeling that is hard to put into words. Those who have dared to take the road know the joy of which I speak.

The most common source of conflict in cells is over the issue of meaningful roles. Ernest Bormann's work at the University of Minnesota with zero-history groups revealed a process of role emergence wherein members vie for certain roles and are either confirmed in these roles or forced to seek another role (Bormann, 1990). Often, if someone wanted to be the leader of the group, but was not confirmed in that role, he or she became a central negative figure and disrupted the process, like Jim in the story about the team at Acme Manufacturing. Healthy cells learn how to expose this issue to the light and deal with it in ways that respect the individual and the group. Most of the time, I have discovered that a meaningful role awaits everyone who is willing to get involved. But both the group and the individual might have to face the truth that sometimes people need to move to another group or cell to find a more meaningful role. The critical factor is to deal openly with the issue and to always respect the person.

PHASE FOUR: PROBLEM SOLVING

An important part of any transformation process is problem solving. It can also be fun. The most important thing for groups or cells to remember as they move in and out of problem solving is to value open dialogue and to look for a rich blend rather than consensus for consensus' sake.

My advice, once again, is to use the theory, structure, script model to facilitate dialogue around the shadows that have grown in the system. It is important to take the facts and shape them into insights. For example, your group might discover from having gathered the facts that the theory about people in your workplace is that they are basically lazy and in need of direction or that the best way to get people to do things is with extrinsic rewards, which generally means money. Perhaps you will discover that the reward system favors those at the top. After further discussion about theories of human behavior, you might conclude that the reason people need extrinsic rewards is that they have never been given a chance to connect their special gifts to the task at hand, and thus experience the joy of work for its own sake. Or that people have become convinced from elementary school on up that we are all creatures motivated by material rewards and status. After further dialogue, you might even conclude that theories about human motivation can be self-fulfilling, that to a certain extent people become what is expected of them. Or you could discover that the very people who seem to lack motivation are highly motivated in other areas of their lives. It could be that the shadows are in the belief system, the theories at work. And that ultimately these theories are manifested in scripts that make it look as if people do not care about their work.

Once groups discover the source of the problem, they can play with solutions and try out different scenarios. In the example used above, what if the group decided to experiment with a project assigned to a self-managed group wherein each person got to choose the role best suited for her talents and interests? If someone was unable to find a fit in one group, he would be allowed to move to another group where his talents and interests fit better.

I know it is not that simple, but the point of this example is to demonstrate that problem-solving dialogue can reveal what is behind the facts and help a group discover ways to change the theories, structures, and scripts into ways that help people shine. More importantly, it can be another way to connect people to a task and a group of others. It can also be fun.

Clouds to Watch Out For in Phase Four

Several clouds can get in the way of the open dialogue that is such an important part of problem solving. Some of them have already been covered, such as the clouds of blame and the clouds of fear. I might add one set that is particularly troublesome in this phase; it is the *clouds of self-protection*.

The clouds of self protection could just as easily have been included with the other clouds of fear. Indeed, their origin is in the fear of losing face. Ernest Becker asserts that rituals of self-protection can be traced back to the fear of death itself, that at a deeper level we equate a put-down with death, with insignificance. Erving Goffman, whom I have quoted throughout this book, shed more light on the issue of self-protection rituals than anyone I know (Goffman, 1959). He reminded us that the self is a very sacred thing in a world in which other sacred symbols have been discredited or destroyed. That is why we strive to protect it at all costs. As Argyris so wisely observed, it is this fear of being embarrassed, caught without a script, that produces the defensive maneuvers that get in the way of healthy change in the organization (Argyris, 1993).

Unfortunately, the clouds of self-protection are hard to break up. It requires a willingness to lose control—perhaps to lose the self in order to find the self. We usually do this only in a safe environment, one where trust is high based on having watched others expose themselves and come out okay. Thus, we are back to the old chicken-and-egg dilemma: which comes first, the healthy trusting environment or people who dare to trust each other? If there is a piece of advice I can offer here it is that practice makes perfect. Certainly, it helps to expose the shadows, even to map out unhealthy scripts so that people can see the error of their ways. It also helps to learn new skills based on empathy and a willingness for self-disclosure, but unless people are truly convinced they will not be put down, they will hesitate to expose parts of themselves. And people become convinced that they will not be put down only when they see others expose themselves to embarrassment and still receive the confirmation of the group. And it really sinks in when they experience it for themselves.

This might sound like an oversimplification, but I have discovered from dealing with this issue—and after making all the classic mistakes—that it helps when people are given opportunities to shine. When we shine we tend to focus our energy on the task and building relationships with others and purposes that transcend the immediate. We have less time to worry about protecting ourselves.

Perhaps there is a lesson to be learned from people like George, the man in my story who was always present for others. When we accept the faults of others in ourselves, confirm others unconditionally, and make ourselves present for each other, we begin to build the trust needed to open up dialogue to a new dimension.

PHASE FIVE: IDEA-FINDING AND PLAYING WITH SOLUTIONS

Groups that move from a place to work to a place to shine also learn how to build upon the healthy interaction within the group and play with ideas and solutions. They have relearned the art of spontaneous involvement—getting lost in the flow of ideas. Some call it serious play, to bring it into the context of the workplace, but I'm not certain that's necessary. After all, play is play. And making it serious takes something out of it.

There are all kinds of ways to introduce play into this phase of a transformation process. I know of groups that have used cartoon characters to help them synthesize ideas. Some groups even use songs and drama to work with ideas in creative ways. They point out that one must use more creative forms of communication to bring out creativity. A common practice among quality teams is to use a "quarter jar." Any time a member of the team breaks a rule, or more importantly, puts someone down, he must toss a quarter into the jar. Soon the quarter jar becomes a way to lighten the conversation and to relieve tension within the group. As long as it does not become a way to avoid dealing with issues, gimmicks like quarter jars can become effective tools, introducing an element of play. However, the most rewarding form of play recorded by effective groups or cells is a spontaneous playing with ideas and solutions that emerges naturally from interaction and open dialogue and leads to synthesis and new solutions.

Cells of people who have taken on the challenge of building places to shine have discovered a healthy balance between the free flow of ideas (sometimes called brainstorming) and the discipline of synthesis (sometimes called planning or process). They have also discovered that the process of stimulating idea generation and uncovering "aha's" and insights is rewarding for its own sake. If done in the spirit of open dialogue where each person's input is encouraged and respected, the process can build trust. Often significant events in the life of the group help group members form a bond during this phase. The bond is frequently reinforced through shared stories and the events become part of the group's shared history. An example may help illuminate this point.

This particular example comes from the story of a group of people who worked in the customer service department of a medium-sized company that made syrups and toppings for things like ice cream. Several people in the company had sensed for a long time that morale was low. Like many of their competitors, they had gone through a quality movement that had resulted in streamlined processes and lots of cross-functional teams. But the result that stuck out the most in the minds of many was the reduction in people. Over fifteen percent of the people who had worked in the company when the quality program started were now gone.

In retrospect, Janet, the person who started the cell, would tell you that the layoffs were the triggering event that convinced everyone, including some in management, that the company was in a mess. People were showing up at work, but their hearts were not in it. And it was beginning to show in the form of conflict between employees, high absenteeism (mostly in the form of sick days) and lots of customer complaints. Profits were up only because of cost cutting. Six months after the layoffs, sales were about as sluggish as the morale of the people who worked there. This was the point at which Janet decided to do something about it.

Along with two other people from customer service and one from sales, Janet formed a cell whose general purpose at the beginning was to improve morale. During the first few meetings, the cell went through the process of agreeing upon roles. Fortunately, Janet emerged as the natural leader and the process went fairly smoothly. They then struggled through the process of bringing different desires into a common blend, while maintaining the integrity of each member's own desires for a better place to work. They used the theory, structure, script model to gather the facts and reveal the clouded thinking, structuring, and acting that were casting shadows. And then they began the process of sharing ideas and searching for workable solutions.

During the phase of ideas and solutions, an event took place that the members of the "morale cell" (the name the group had given themselves) now share frequently. It happened when the group decided to share their early findings with the VP of Sales and Marketing, who was Janet's boss. When they pointed out the shadows that they had discovered in the theories, structures, and scripts of the organization, Janet's boss responded by bringing in the clouds of minimization. He suggested that the group's findings were inconclusive and speculative. He further suggested that the cell was stealing time from their "regular jobs" and hurting productivity. Janet decided to take a risk and confronted her boss, asking him to produce specific details to back his allegations. She suggested that if he could not see the value of improved morale, the group was more than willing to meet on their own time, after work or on weekends. Following her remarks, Janet noticed the members of the group looking at her as if she were already history. But a strange thing happened. Janet's boss was impressed with her passion and he agreed to a compromise whereby the group could meet over lunch. He even agreed to attend a meeting now and then himself. To this day the group talks about "the great confrontation," in reference to Janet's stand against her boss, with a feeling of pride.

The example above shows how a specific event in the process of sharing ideas and trying out solutions can form a bond within a group of people. In this case the confrontation with Janet's boss became a focal event for the group and a story around which they could discuss other issues within the group. Janet's boss became a villain figure, now reformed, and Janet herself became a hero figure to the group. This is consistent with research on small groups that has shown that groups will create fantasies with heroes and villains, even if they have to create them from another time and place (Bormann, 1990). It is a way for the group to deal with the tension of working together and to discover shared values that shape the norms for behavior in the task, as well as the relationship dimensions of the group.

Playing with ideas and finding new solutions is an important phase of the creative process in the transformation of a system. Perhaps these findings are consistent with the work of sociologists like George Herbert Mead, who proposed that humans learn by playing at new roles, and the studies by Gergen referred to earlier that show how play is an important part of overcoming the fear of change and learning to come up with new ways to relate (Gergen, 1984).

Ah, but as my more left-brain friends would remind me, there must be a way to bring discipline to play. Otherwise ideas won't turn into solutions. I must admit they are right. And in truth, I have discovered tools do help bring discipline—as long as the tool doesn't get in the way of playing with new ideas and roles. One tool that I have found to be rather effective is often called the *bull's-eye*. It is a way to bring visions and beliefs into practice and turn them into new behaviors. It looks something like the figure below.

Bull's-Eye Approach

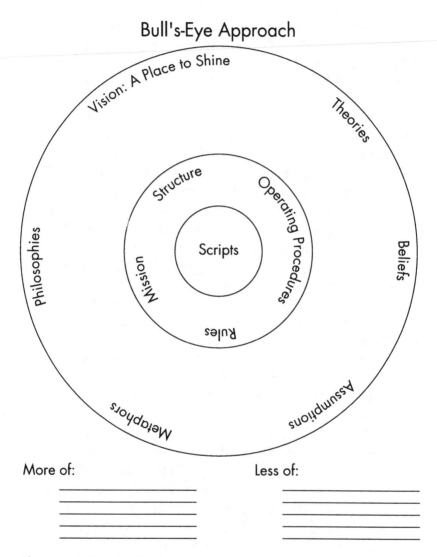

Figure 16–1   Bull's-Eye Approach

At the outer ring of the bull's-eye is a vision of a healthier workplace, in this case a place to shine, along with the theories, beliefs, and assumptions about people, work, and organizations. In the second ring are comments about structure, including mission statements, standard operating procedures, and rules. The comments about structure should show how it facilitates people connecting to purposes and other people. The center ring, which is the bull's-eye, is the place for scripts, the "doing" dimension. To support these scripts with real behaviors, the model leaves room at the bottom to list the behaviors that will support the vision, beliefs, and structures of a place to shine. It is a simple way for the group to get at the behaviors needed to support their vision without losing sight of the underlying beliefs and the structures that support people connecting to their work and each other, and to articulate how their work connects to purposes that transcend the immediate. It forces the group to turn theories and structures into solutions and actions. Most groups or cells adapt this simple model to fit their needs and to encourage open dialogue around specific ideas and solutions. Again, it is not a perfect model. I am sure you can come up with a better one, but in any case, models like this one can be an especially effective tool for encouraging reflection and action and then connecting the two.

The important thing to remember in the idea- and solution-finding phase of the process is that there are no perfect solutions. There are, however, solutions that promote connecting people to purposes and each other and those that lead to alienation, a pitting of the organization against its people. If you look for solutions that promote the former or fit the definition of a place to shine, you are heading in the right direction. And if you are heading in the right direction, the process itself—especially the play of ideas and solutions and the discovery of meaningful roles—will serve to connect people to their work and each other in ways that are confirming and consistent with the concepts of a place to shine.

Clouds to Watch Out For in Phase Five

Clouds are cumulative. That is to say, the clouds that appear in one phase or event of a transformation process can and will appear in another phase. Therefore, all of the clouds that emerge in the first four phases can also emerge in the idea- and solution-finding phase. In addition to the clouds already cited in the first four phases, I will add two more to watch out for here.

The first set I call *serious clouds*. Serious clouds get in the way of play and keep the group from experiencing the fun of working with ideas and sharing insights. Worse yet, they interfere with the healthy process of playing at new roles and learning to cope with new ways of relating to work and each other. I am not talking about throwing out the discipline of good decision-making habits. Indeed, a group can be very disciplined and practical and still have fun. True artists remind me that every form of art has its rules, whether it is writing music or playing baseball. Knowing the rules and learning how to play within the guidelines of a process can make things even more fun, as long as one remains flexible and does not let the process rule the interaction of ideas and solutions. The point is that there is no need for people to be serious all of the time or to be serious just because they are at work or the job is difficult. Play is a healthy way to deal with change. What's more, a little laughter goes a long way toward alleviating the pressure of a seemingly insurmountable task.

The second set of clouds I will add here are *clouds of polarization*. In the solution-finding phase, it is so easy to latch onto a solution and not let go. That's why play is so important in this phase. The more we learn to enjoy the process itself, the more we will avoid the impulse to stick our feet in cement. But I also know that it is not that easy to change defensive rituals.

My advice for avoiding clouds of polarization is to practice the art of play, but also to build trust through open interaction. It goes back to learning how to deal with conflict openly and to learn from differences. There are techniques and programs for doing this, ranging all the way from mapping out unhealthy scripts so that people can see them, to learning the skills of empathy, open dialogue, self-disclosure, and straight talk. The important thing is to recognize the shadows cast by these clouds and to agree upon a way to deal with them. Whatever method is chosen, the group must agree to buy into it before it will work.

PHASE SIX: ACCEPTANCE-FINDING AND CONFIRMATION

The final phase or critical event that is part of the process of transforming a place to work into a place to shine is acceptance-finding and confirmation. In fact, this phase might be one of the most important. In other words, I might have saved the best for last.

Phase six is important because it happens throughout the process. As I stated upfront, the process of creative transformation is a circular one that goes on and on and jumps from phase to phase in a very nonlinear fashion. For example, a group or cell might find themselves brainstorming ideas one day and taking time out to confirm a decision the next, only to skip back to problem solving the following day. New theories, structures, and scripts must be accepted as a way of life as the group struggles with change. The process of acceptance and confirmation is ongoing and gives the group the opportunity to take time out and celebrate their accomplishments, and reconfirm the value of each member to the whole.

Acceptance and confirmation of a decision or working through the struggle for roles can be important events that help a group form a common bond. Often, new symbols are born in the process of acceptance and confirmation. In the case of the transformation of the systems and culture of a country, this means new heroes, a new flag, or a new national anthem. In the case of the workplace it could mean a new motto or theme like "We Care," the theme that emerged in my own division, or "The Morale Cell," the name the customer service group in the story I told earlier gave themselves. Heroes themselves can become symbols of a new culture or a movement, as in the case of Martin Luther King, Jr., in the civil rights movement or Nelson Mandela in the South African struggle against apartheid.

Ernest Bormann called the process of moving from a bunch of people to a cohesive group a process of *symbolic conversion*, to emphasize the point that symbols in the form of heroes, stories, slogans, and artifacts begin to take on meaning as people struggle with roles and relationships between the members of the group, learn the norms or acceptable behaviors toward each other and the task, and learn from conflict. He emphasized the need to celebrate small victories in the process, to solidify acceptance of the idea, solution, or decision, and to reconfirm each member in the process. It is a critical part of the process of transforming a place to work into a place to shine. If it is missing, the group never seems to achieve its potential.

Clouds to Watch Out For in Phase Six

I was tempted to refer to all of the previous clouds and leave it at that. After all, they apply here as well as in the other phases. And I felt that I had pretty much covered the bases. But after reflecting further on the importance of acceptance and confirmation, I decided to add one more set of clouds. I call them *clouds of complacency.*

Clouds of complacency tend to block out the need to keep the process going. They send a message that it is over just because things seem to be better. If we don't watch out, clouds of complacency can grow until we fall asleep in the shadows again. Worse still, clouds of complacency can keep us from sending messages of appreciation and confirmation to each other and destroy the energy that builds in a cell of people who care for each other and their work. The best way to avoid clouds of complacency is to take time out and ask the members of the group how they feel, or to revisit the vision, using the theory, structure, script model, and ask yourself if people are truly shining.

SOME FINAL THOUGHTS ABOUT CELLS AND PROCESSES

If we are going to build places to shine we must do it together. I have suggested that one form to consider is that of a cell—a group of people who blend their passion into a common force. In an effort to help us get our arms around the process of forming a cell and making it work, I have offered a model with phases or critical events, and shared what I and others have learned about the clouds that can get in the way of emerging from the shadows and moving from a place to work to a place to shine. I hope that I have made it clear that articulating the right set of phases or events or dispelling all of the right clouds is not the important thing here. Rather, it is the process itself and the magic of bringing new light into our work through connecting to others around a common vision of a healthier place to work and to love. To bring this point home, I will close with some final thoughts.

Some change consultants would have us believe that people form a bond around a clear vision or a shared goal. Therefore, they say, it is important for leaders to articulate clear visions and goals. No doubt it is important to have clear visions and goals, but Bormann, along with other experts in small-group behavior, suggests that, contrary to what we have been taught to believe, members of a group congregate around common means with differing goals, desires, and agendas, out of which emerge common missions, visions, and goals, sometimes for only limited periods of time. James March developed a theory around the concept of goals and solutions coming together called *garbage can theory* and suggested that organizations comprise problems and solutions that come together around critical events and deadlines like the annual budgeting process (Cohen, March and Olsen, 1972). These thoughts, along with the evidence that I and others have accumulated over the years from watching work groups, imply that it is more important for leaders to inspire a group with their own passion and help each member of the group find a meaningful role than it is to articulate the perfect vision.

What the experts referred to above don't tell us about, at least not so that it is obvious, is the secret ingredient that seems to be present in almost every real-life example of a transformation from a place to work to a place to shine. It is an ingredient that I have experienced and felt in my heart working with the division that cared and that I have watched emerge in other groups or cells of people. A word that begins to describe this secret ingredient is passion, but that doesn't go far enough. It is an energy force, a source of light in the shadows, that seems to build within the members of the cell as well as between them. Thus, it includes a passion for the task at hand, but it is also includes a compassion for others. Martin Buber felt this energy and invented his own word for it. He called it the power of an *inbetweenness*. He noted that it emerges when we lose ourselves in a relationship and confirm the potential in each other. I doubt that I could come up with a better way to say it than Buber. All I know is that it is an energy that I felt in the division that cared and experienced again as I observed a flavor company in Ohio, a cheese plant in Wisconsin, and an information services company in Tennessee. I suspect that this same energy source is alive in companies like Southwest Airlines that seem to do well in industries where they should never survive under the normal rules of the game. I suspect that it is an energy that many people have tasted and don't quite know how to describe.

In my opinion, if there is one thing we can do as individuals and as caring cells of people that will make a real difference in our work and bring about places to shine, it is to tap into the energy of inbetweenness. Some call it a spiritual force that emerges from inside as well as outside of us—a source of light that gives us the power to emerge from the shadows within us and those we have built into our systems, such as those found in the organizations where we work. No one is certain what the organizations of the future will look like or exactly what will be contained in the final terms and conditions of the new social contract between people, their work, and the organizations where they work. But no matter what form it takes, there must be room for caring cells of people to emerge and tap into a source of light. This source of light is discovered when we connect around purposes that transcend the immediate—like building a better world for those who will follow us—and share it with others who care.

17

Leadership in a New Light

> Superior leaders are those whose existence is merely known;
> The next best are loved and honored;
> The next are respected;
> And the next are ridiculed.
> Those who lack belief
> Will not in turn be believed.
> But when the command comes from afar
> And the work is done, the goal achieved,
> The people say, "We did it naturally."
>
> from *The Tao of Power*
> ... by R. W. WING

I once vowed that I would never write about leadership. So much has been written already that there is nothing new left to say about it. Minneapolis playwright and journalist Syl Jones, who is never afraid to speak candidly about such issues, expressed my feelings well in an editorial in the June 17, 1995 issue of the *Minneapolis Star Tribune* when he wrote: "Leadership is that elusive quality that blends wisdom with humility. As such, it is a commodity more scarce than precious metals and perhaps more valuable, which explains why so many gurus today are trying to create leadership the way the alchemists of old concocted gold— in a flash."

It seems to me that we have demeaned the role of leader by batting around theories and dishing out recipes for behavior as if they can be cooked up overnight. We even throw around terms like "soul" and "spirituality" as if they too are nothing more than coffee talk. We imply that anyone can be a leader simply by taking on the right attitude and practicing the right habits. But those who have taken the call seriously know that real leadership involves more than learning the latest theory and adopting a new set of habits. Real leadership emerges the old-fashioned way, by rolling up our sleeves and getting lost in the task and the people.

Does this mean we should throw out all the theories about leadership? Although I am ready to do just that some days, I know that's not the real answer. I also know that in spite of my belief that real leaders are rare, we need real leaders if we are going to build healthier relationships at work and help people shine. Indeed, during these times of chaos and lost identities at work, we need real leaders more than ever. That's why I opened this book with a special note for leaders. But where do real leaders come from, and how will we know who they are when they do show themselves? To get at the answer, maybe we need to take another look at leadership, this time in a new light.

It seems to me that there are four major schools of thought about the concept of leadership. A quick look at them may help us appreciate the complexity of the concept and provide insight.

The first and perhaps the oldest set of theories about leadership are the *trait theories*. These are also known as the *great person* theories. They are based on the notion of the born leader. The idea is that some people are blessed with the natural traits to be leaders. R. M. Stogdill summarized years of research based on the idea that certain traits predispose the people who possess them to emerge as leaders more than others (Stogdill, 1974). Some of the findings were interesting, such as the discovery that height, weight, and intelligence correlate to formal leadership. However, the results were inconclusive at best, based on inconsistent and contradictory findings.

Anthropologist Ernest Becker reminds us that the trait approach goes back to our tribal roots and the need for heroes, people who represented the ability to transcend the natural forces of life and death. Later, this same need for power over the forces of death resulted in our willingness to connect to powerful people, groups, or ideologies. It was given new life during the days of the divine right of rulers, the remnants of which still influence our thinking. Becker would say that modern-day heroes are around in the form of movie stars, sports heroes, and successful executives of major corporations, people who seem to live forever because of their accomplishments.

The trait theory of leadership is important to note since it helps to explain the loyalty of followers to leaders even when they lead in the wrong direction. If we connect Becker's ideas to the phenomenon of transference advanced by Freud, wherein the patient transfers the role of parent or significant other to the therapist, we begin to understand even more clearly why people seek so hard to receive the approval of the boss at work. Wise leaders are aware of the awesome power they hold in their hands because of this and treat that power with care, while enabling those who choose to follow them to develop wings to fly under their own power.

The second school of thought about leadership concerns the *style theories.* This thinking grew out of the industrial era and the emergence of the professional manager. Style theories say that leadership can be learned. All one has to do is to learn the right attitude, practice the right skills, and relate in the right ways to the followers. The social sciences helped promote these theories. For example, the results of the famous studies of Lippit and White in the 50s with teenagers at a camp were transferred to the workplace (Olmsted and Hare, 1978). Three styles of leadership were studied: *authoritarian, democratic,* and *laissez faire.* Based on the results, the democratic style was promoted as the best style under most situations, although the tough leaders in the organizations across America never bought into this "soft" advice. Later, more enlightened consultants and leaders advocated a *participative* style, based on the notion of becoming a participator in the task with the workers. However, this concept was often interpreted as a way to delegate or "dump" work to a level below. Furthermore, the studies that tried to prove the validity of participative styles were inconclusive (Bormann, 1990). Nevertheless, enlightened leaders still sensed that getting people to participate in the process of decision-making would result in more buy-in and motivation to accomplish goals. The questions that remained unanswered were: number one, how do you convince people to want to get involved, and number two, when do you get them involved without compromising the quality of the decision? Contingency theorists came forth with the variables to help answer the second question, but even their elaborate formulas did not clear up the issues and tradeoffs.

More recently, a new offshoot, based on style-theory thinking, that leadership can be taught has become quite popular. Some of this is billed under the label of ethical leadership; others refer to it as "soulful" or even "spiritual." Although these theories differ in their approach, with more of an emphasis on the cognitive process of experience and reflection, they are still based on the idea that leadership is a skill, a set of attitudes, or an awareness that can be learned. It is also important to point out that many of the modern theories have added the importance of acknowledging forces outside of our control and the importance of creating visions and building relationships.

The third set of theories about leadership are *contingency theories.* Also known as situational theories, the thinking behind these theories is that styles of leadership are not set for all time; rather, leaders must adapt their styles to the situation, both the task and the people. Researchers in this area looked at every variable capable of being measured, including the difficulty of the task, the number of decision paths, the maturity of the people, the stability of the environment, and the type of products and services offered (Perrow, 1986). Like the other three, these theories provided valuable insights into the art of leadership. In this case, the need to adjust to the situation and to consider multiple variables added valuable knowledge to our understanding of leadership as an art rather than a science.

Many leaders I know who tried to apply the contingency model discovered a simple truth: Don't try to be someone you are not. Michael Maccoby's research on social types shed light on this point. He noted five social types in the modern corporation: experts, helpers, defenders, innovators, and self-developers. While it is important to improve on weaknesses and to be able to adapt to situations, followers will see through someone who is trying to be someone he is not. For example, the worst thing a helper-leader can do is try to pretend he is a defender or to suddenly become an innovator. If the change does not come from the heart, people will see right through it. Yet leaders who admit their shortcomings, attempt to learn new skills and perspectives, and aren't afraid to tap into the strengths of others, actually grow in power. They discover that real power comes from reflecting and acting and one becomes the most powerful when one makes others powerful. The best advice I can give is to be honest with yourself and to use the strengths of others where you have weaknesses. In other words, be yourself.

The final set of theories I wish to briefly review emerged from the study of small work groups. Bormann calls it *contextual leadership theory* (Bormann, 1990). The theory combines the insights from the other three theories and adds the process to the blend. Observing small task-oriented groups of students who had no previous history of working together, Bormann discovered that leaders emerge from a process of role emergence within the group. He called it a process of *residue* to emphasize its evolving nature and to show that leaders emerge from a process of elimination. Those who are not qualified or do not establish credibility in the eyes of the followers do not become natural leaders.

The process Bormann observed involves two phases and four patterns. Phase one was an elimination of the unfit, those whose early overtures were rejected by the group because they came on too strong or appeared less than knowledgeable about the task. The second phase was a bit messier. It involved a struggle between two or more contenders for the role of leader. In one pattern observed, a single leader emerged after a brief struggle between two contenders. The one who did not emerge as leader found a meaningful role as an expert or a defender of the cause, sort of a Ralph Nader of the group. In another pattern, a leader emerged as a result of a crisis in the group. In still another pattern, two contenders continued to struggle for the role of leader throughout the life of the group and the struggle was never resolved. The story about Jim and Al from Acme Manufacturing in Chapter 14 provides an example of this pattern. Bormann's findings, based on responses from members of the groups actually involved in the studies, suggest that the more productive and fun groups were those in which a leader emerged rather quickly and held the role for an extended period of time.

Do these same patterns unfold in the workplace? Bormann and others think that they do, but that they are mediated by the power of the hierarchy and the myths of the organization about heroes and villains. Although the studies of contextual leadership theory in the workplace are limited, the results suggest that leaders also emerge in the organizations based on this same process of contenders vying for the role and being either accepted or rejected by the group. In the case of the formal organizational structure, however, the assigning of leaders and placing positional power in the role itself prevents some of the natural process of leader emergence from unfolding. Nonetheless, the phenomenon occurs, which helps explain the presence of informal structures and why, in some cases, the formal appointed leader is only a figurehead and the natural leader of the group is someone else, often another member of the group.

We learn from contextual leadership theory just as we can learn from other theories. For one thing, we can learn that all great leaders have one thing in common: followers. More importantly, we can begin to appreciate that leaders emerge from a process of interacting with people around a task or a performance.

Furthermore, they must prove to the group that they are worthy of the calling. This could lead one to the tentative conclusion that leaders are only as good as the followers make them. Perhaps then the real issue is not leadership, but followership. The issue then would be: how do we educate followers to discern real leadership potential when they see it so that they can enable the leader to lead and promote the healthy development of the entire group? Perhaps an approach would be to consider the kinds of experiences and learning that need to take place in order for both followers and leaders to work together to build places to shine.

Perhaps I have tipped the scale too far in favor of the power of followers to shape leaders. If nothing else, I have raised the ageless sociological question: Is it the great person that creates the great society or the great society that creates the great person? Or is this one of those wonderful paradoxes with an ambiguous answer? Do they, as Erving Goffman surmised, really "grow up together" (Goffman, 1961)?

An expert on adult education, Patricia Cross, introduced a metaphor to help deal with this dilemma in the educational system. She compared teaching and learning to cooking and eating food. The teachers were the cooks, the ones who dished out the meals, and the students felt obligated to eat what was placed in front of them or reject it. Cross suggested another alternative. If the students began to demand gourmet meals, the cooks would be forced to cook better. Or if the cooks prepared gourmet food, perhaps the students would learn to eat and love it. If I were to apply this metaphor to the workplace, I would say that leaders and followers must work together to cook up a new menu.

Maybe there is another way to look at this. We all know that we need leaders, people who are willing to accept the call to go the extra mile and care for the task and the people. We also know that these leaders are more effective when they are chosen by the group. And we know that great leaders share certain qualities that emerge in times when they are needed the most. But most of all we know that leadership is about relationships and interaction. Great leaders are born out of the process of interacting with others around differing goals and aspirations that come together in a rich blend to achieve a common purpose. Therefore, leadership is really about interacting. Once again, we are back to the concept of "inbetweenness," the energy that emerges from relationships. Perhaps I am only talking in circles, but my experience tells me that great leaders will emerge when we all take responsibility for building places to shine. Leadership and followership are inseparable concepts. We won't have great leaders if we do not have great followers.

What are the qualities of leaders and followers who bring about places to shine? The shelves are full of books that offer answers to this question. In fact, there are so many answers that it can be confusing at times. I don't need to duplicate the work of others or add to the confusion. I would, however, offer a couple of thoughts based on the experience and wisdom of those who do not profess to have the answers, but offer the right questions to stimulate the dialogue this issue deserves.

One of the wise leaders of our century was Robert Greenleaf, author of *Servant Leadership* (Greenleaf, 1977). He tried to capture some of these qualities in his book. I will share his thoughts as best I can and add a few of my own.

The first quality of a wise leader, as Greenleaf saw it, was *beauty*. Greenleaf referred to the mathematical definition of the word "beauty," making reference to the concept of penetrating the unknown, daring to get lost in the task and the people. To me, to be blessed with the quality of beauty is to have the capacity to play with new ideas and to let them speak to us in new ways. It fits well into the part of the natural process of transformation that I referred to as phase four: "idea-finding and playing with solutions." I would add to Greenleaf's thinking another concept borrowed from Martin Buber and already referred to: "making present." I define it as the capacity to go beyond empathy, to dare to get to know someone at a level where you experience their pain, including the pain you might be causing them just by being human. It is a capacity that great leaders and followers possess that enables them to understand where they shine and thus to help others discover a way to shine. A willingness to make others present through listening and caring can act as a buffer against the intoxicating effect of the power of leadership. I have discovered that if we are truly connected to people to the extent that we are present for them, we will no longer be able to hide behind the invisible shield of the organization and treat people as human resources. The people will be our judge and it will not be easy to let them down. We will be accountable to each other. A scary proposition indeed, but I see no alternative if we are to be bold leaders and followers who build places to shine.

The second quality of wise leaders cited by Greenleaf is *momentaneity*. It is the quality of being able to see the opportunity to shine in each moment. Referring to the qualities of Nelson Mandela and other leaders who emerged in the struggle to transform South Africa, Kobus Neethling cited the quality of *anti-negativity*. I think he was getting at the same thing. Wise leaders know the importance of inspiring the group to see the opportunities before them, to sense the light inside of them and around them in spite of the clouds that force their way into the process. The psalmist described this quality with the words: "This is the day which the Lord hath made, rejoice and be glad in it." Emerson recognized the quality with his own words: "He is rich who owns the day." Wise leaders have learned to be open to the moment. They are willing to embrace the shadows, but they are farsighted enough to see the light within, between, and around those with whom they work.

Hand in hand with the capacity for momentaneity is what Charles Handy called the *capacity for living with paradox* (Handy, 1994). Indeed, I will offer a paradox of my own to make my point. Great leaders and followers are able to see the opportunity in a situation, but they also have, to use Handy's phrase, a *negative capacity*. They can live with things being out of sorts for a while. They have learned that it is more important to let a question live than to kill it for the sake of completing a task or keeping a false peace. They have learned that the process of transformation will not unfold without a willingness to embrace the shadows and a trust in the self-organizing patterns in chaos itself. Which leads me to the next quality cited by Greenleaf: *openness.*

Openness is the capacity to learn from ideas that differ from your own. Wise leaders and followers know that people learn and grow from the sharing of diverse ideas. They are aware of the natural inclination to let a question die just because it sounds dumb or threatens their status and they guard against bringing closure before it is time just because someone needs a decision at once. Indeed, wise leaders and followers welcome challenge and nurture dialogue. They have learned that this is how truth emerges, and more importantly, how people realize their true potential. Like Martin Buber, wise leaders and followers have discovered that the self becomes stronger through interaction with others. They know from experience that we are found by our place to shine when we lose ourselves in a relationship to our work and each other.

Greenleaf cited another quality of wise leaders: *humor.* Wise leaders and followers delight in playing with ideas and watching people realize their potential. They know the healing power of laughter firsthand. As my wise mentor said, "The joy is in the building." Wise leaders and followers practice the art of play in the spirit of humor that encourages people to work, love, and play all in the same place.

The final quality mentioned by Greenleaf is *tolerance.* I think he was referring to the quality of accepting the human condition in oneself as well as others. Why is it that many of our great leaders and followers have emerged from experiences in prisons or from being victims of a system that punishes those who will not go along with the tide? I hesitated to make this next statement for fear it would sound like I am promoting a martyr syndrome. But I will say it anyway because I think it needs to be said. Wise leaders and followers that I have known have suffered. They have exposed themselves to living and been wounded in the process. Moreover, they have learned to shine from their wounds. The fact is, to live is to be wounded—that is, if we have dared to live at all. In the words of the ancient Portuguese proverb: "Die young or suffer much." The secret is to learn from our wounds. My son, Troy, who is a physician, reminds me that the tougher parts of our physical bodies are the places where we have healed and formed scar tissue or new bone structure. I think the same is true for our hearts and souls. In the words of Nietzsche, "What does not destroy me, makes me stronger" (Kaufmann, 1976).

How do wise leaders acquire qualities like those cited by Greenleaf? Are they born with them or do they learn them by adopting the right style and applying it to the right situation? I think not. I think wise leaders become wise by leading, making mistakes, learning from them, and from listening to those who have called them to lead.

This chapter has already grown beyond my original intent, but I feel compelled to share a quote from William Foster. Commenting on the need for a new pedagogy on leadership, he writes:

> Leadership, in the final analysis, is the ability of humans to relate deeply to each other in the search for a more perfect union. Leadership is a consensual task, a sharing of ideas and a sharing of responsiblities, where a 'leader' is a leader for the moment only, where the leadership exerted must be validated by the consent of the followers, and where leadership lies in the struggles of a community to find meaning for itself (Foster, 1992).

As we take on the challenge to transform the workplace from a place to work into a place to shine, and expose our theories, structures, and scripts to a new light, our ideas about leadership will change as well. I hope that we will move beyond the top-down, command-control models of leadership. I hope we will be forced to look at leadership as a concept that captures the interaction between people in search of a better world and leaders as people who choose to fill a role that emerges from the process of interacting around a task, where people care and confirm each other in the spirit of the community. We will begin to appreciate that leadership is as much about following as it is about leading, that leaders become what we expect of them.

The truth is, the forces of change in the workplace will redefine leadership along with other relationships at work whether
we want them to or not. In the meantime, leaders in organizations
will continue to appoint others like themselves. Some will emerge
as leaders chosen by the group, while others will not. Informal
leaders will continue to emerge from groups of people who care
for their work and each other. Cells will emerge around people
and purposes. And as always, the real leaders will probably be
less visible than those who would take the credit. But we will know
they have been there. Why? Because the work was done and "we
did it naturally."

A Quiet Power

> There's no room for self-pity in the lived life.
> Only the unlived quality of our existence
> should ever make us sad.
>
> .... GERHARD FROST

"I'm not sure when I became a leader or if I ever became
one. I only know the work got done and people seemed
to have fun." Such were the words of a woman I interviewed not long ago. Her story sends a loud message
about real leadership.

I will call her Alice, although that is not her real
name. Her "official" role in the organization is to su-
pervise a group of customer service representatives.
Alice would never say this if she were writing this piece,
but customer service is a thankless job. People who
work in customer service receive all the complaints, but
seldom get any of the credit. Yet as any seasoned man-

ager would attest, they are the backbone of the business, the point at which the company or institution meets the customer. This is an irony born of the hierarchical structure of the industrial era that has yet to be corrected. Those who are most critical to the part of the chain that links the product to the customer are often the least respected and rewarded.

Alice didn't seem to mind not getting the credit due her. On the other hand, when it came to the people in her department, the story was different. Alice would fight tooth and nail to make sure that the sales reps and marketing gurus knew who made the business tick. She made certain that the members of her team were given roles on cross-functional teams when they wanted them. She would nominate them for rewards and make certain that they were recognized whenever and wherever she could influence the decision makers of the company. But that is not the reason the people in the customer service department loved and respected Alice. To discover the answer to that question one needed to talk to them. So I did.

What I discovered from the people in customer service who reported to Alice was both interesting and enlightening. I knew that Alice was one of those rare leaders who got things done while helping her people shine and find joy in their work, but I expected different answers to my questions about why that was so than the ones I received.

There was one word that came up over and over again when I asked about Alice. The word was "real." One of the customer service reps put it this way: "Alice is not perfect by any stretch of the imagination, but she knows her faults and owns them. She is human and makes us feel okay about being human." Another rep said the same thing a little differently: "Alice does not put on a show; she is the most genuine person I know—faults and all. It just makes me want to work with her."

Another phrase I heard used frequently to describe Alice was "She is always there for us." When I probed further I was told story after story about how Alice was available to help with issues relating to work as well as personal issues and relationships among the group. But as one man put it: "She is there, but not there." He described for me how Alice never interferes unless she needs to. Everyone told me about Alice's uncanny sense of knowing when to make her presence known and when not to.

"Alice listens" was another common phrase used to describe her. It went along with the other attributes I was hearing about Alice. What amazed the people in her group the most was her willingness to listen even when they knew she did not have the time, but most of all, that she would make others who were higher up the ladder in the organization wait so that she could attend to a need of a member in the group. But this quality did not stop within the group. Like the other qualities Alice exhibited, it spread to other groups through the people she was "there for" when they needed someone to listen. Indeed, I suspect that the ripple effect of her willingness to listen spread farther than any of us will ever know, because it inspired others to listen.

"We have fun here" was another phrase I heard spoken often. I was not surprised to hear it. I could tell that from being a part of the group for only a short time.

They worked and played together to the extent that one could not tell the difference. Even during times of conflict between members of the group there was a willingness to laugh at oneself. Watching them, I was reminded of playing tiger in the alfalfa patch as a child. Yet their work always got done and the praise for their service never stopped.

"Forgiveness" is a word that was never said, but it was part of their life together. It was a quality that played itself out in the interaction I observed within the group and between the group and other groups in the company. It went hand in hand with another quality that permeated the group: tolerance. The group seemed to have mastered the fine art of balancing respect for the individual with the needs of the task and the group. I saw people shining who probably would have been put down in other groups, people who lacked the social graces of members from some of the other, more sophisticated groups in the company, or people whose appearance might deceive one into thinking they were not "sharp." Nothing could have been farther from the truth. This was probably the sharpest and the shiniest group of people I had ever encountered.

There was one other quality that permeated the customer service department. I can only describe it as "caring." Each member seemed to care for the others as well as the whole of the group. Not in a siege-mentality way—indeed, the group worked hard to avoid in-group behaviors by encouraging members to work on cross-functional teams and inviting other groups from marketing, sales, credit, and other functions to their staff meetings. They had even piloted a team approach, combining members from all disciplines to serve the customer better. Yet they understood each other and cared for each other in a special, unobtrusive way that showed in their behavior on and off the job. This caring showed itself in incidents like the time that Alice stayed overnight with a member of the group who had lost her spouse. Or when one of the group members cried with Alice into the evening hours over the news that she had developed a cancer (which was later cured).

It was interesting to me that Alice never called herself a leader once during the days that I spent interviewing and observing her and the customer service group. But it was obvious that she was. Because everyone in her sphere of influence experienced the joy of working and loving in the same place. They knew firsthand what it was like to work in a place to shine. And at the end of the day, the work got done.

18

Seven Bold Steps Toward Your Own Place to Shine

I wonder what is going to
be your next step in life:
I think of it and
even pray for it.
May you find the path
which will lead you to
the highest and truest
of yourself!
Keep the right path upwards
and hope for perpetual
discovery–
and trust life
That's all.

> . . . TEILHARD DE CHARDIN

Since I already broke my vow to never write about leadership,
I might as well go one more step and break another vow I once
made never to give advice about the perfect steps to happiness or
any other desirable state—including a place to shine. I made this

183

second vow after reading the umpteenth book about how to discover the perfect life through reflection or how to adapt all the right habits that would lead to happiness. I also wasn't going to give a lot of personal advice in a book that is primarily focused on changing the culture at work. But people kept asking me for personal advice anyway. Furthermore, I know that making changes like those I have suggested, including emerging from the shadows at work and building places to shine, requires both personal reflection and action and the combined efforts of groups in the workplace. Thus, I have decided to offer some advice, but it is qualified advice.

Unlike what we have been led to believe by the quick-fix gurus of our time, changes in the way we think, structure, and act, whether at a personal level or an organizational level, come about after a lot of hard work. What's more, they must be experienced at a much deeper level than many of the formulas out there would suggest. Therefore, the first qualifier I submit is that the steps to a healthier life only get us started. Like a game I played when I was young called "seven steps," the advice I offer here is only intended to give you a head start on being discovered by your own places to shine. Let me explain what I am trying to say by telling you a little more about this game I used to play.

Seven steps was a simple little game with simple rules. The objective of the game was to make it all the way around an object, such as a building or a stack of hay bales, without being seen moving. There was one exception, however. Everyone was given seven free steps to get started on his journey. As in most simple games, one person was "it." This person tried to catch the others moving as they made their way around the building. If you were caught moving, that is making any motion at all, as judged by the person who was "it," you were forced to start over again. Every time you started over you were given another free seven steps.

Seven steps may not be the perfect metaphor or analogy that I was looking for to help show people how to emerge from the shadows at work and build places to shine—including their own place to shine—but the idea of steps as ways to get started can be a healthy metaphor nonetheless. Too often we look at steps as the end all, the answer to life's dilemmas. On the other hand, if we look at steps as pieces of advice to help us get started on our own journeys, we will begin to see a more accurate picture of how life really works. No one can give us the perfect steps or habits to follow that guarantee our lives will be richer. We can only give each other what we have learned from our own journeys and hope that it will help us get started. Just like the game seven steps, no others can walk us through life; they can only give us some advice based on the steps that helped them get started on their own journeys.

In the game of seven steps, I discovered that it helps to make those first seven steps bold ones. It caught the person who was "it" off guard and set the right stage for making it around the building. Therefore, I am going to offer seven bold steps to help you get started on your journey out from the shadows of the organization. But remember! This is only advice. How you discover ways to emerge from the shadows at work and build places to shine is really up to you.

There is one more thing to share about this model before I start. It is upside down. In other words, the model starts at the top and moves toward the bottom; it is much different from the models for success that we are used to seeing. I did this on purpose in order to make a point—especially for leaders. If we hope to emerge from the shadows at work and build healthier relationships with our work and each other, we must "get our heads out of the clouds," so to speak, and begin to make the right connections. The "right" connections I am referring to are not the influential people who can help us land the next promotion. Rather, they are the sacred connections to our work, each other, and purposes that transcend the immediate, the stuff I have been writing about throughout this text. This will require that we move out of our private offices and our private lives and become engaged in our work and with each other. We will never make the "right" connections sitting in our offices. We need to be willing to stand up and take some bold steps toward reconnecting. Figure 18-1 shows seven bold steps that helped me shine. Perhaps they will be of help as you struggle to take those first steps of your own.

Seven Bold Steps

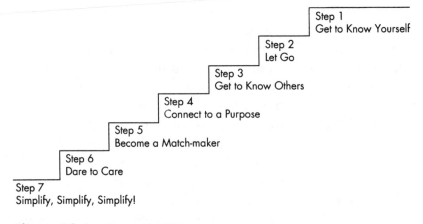

Figure 18-1   Seven Bold Steps

STEP #1: GET TO KNOW YOURSELF

I discovered that the first step I needed to take if I was going to emerge from the shadows and move toward a place to shine was to learn more about myself.

At first I was convinced that the process of getting to know myself would be a complicated one. Consequently, I exposed myself to all the best tools. I studied the personality types based on the work of Jung and translated later into the Myers-Briggs personality types. I exposed myself to the wisdom of the ancient mystics of the Moslem faith, the Sufi's, who used nine personality types called *enneagrams* to describe the special gifts of each person and to teach that one's gift is also one's curse. I looked at all kinds of learning styles and social types. It was a wonderful journey and a fruitful one. But at the end of my "personal work" I discovered a truth more profound for me than all the truths I had discovered in the arts and sciences based on personality and social types. I discovered that the real truths about myself were uncovered in the process itself. And they weren't nearly as complicated as I had thought.

Psychologist Carl Rogers reminds us that the self is not a fixed thing that is over and done with when we are born—something we are stuck with our entire lives. Rather, the self is discovered in one's past, present, and future experiences. Becoming a person, according to Rogers, is a "living, breathing, feeling, fluctuating process" (Rogers, 1961). The self is comfortably lodged in our experiences. We discover ourselves when we let our experiences tell us about who we are becoming. We cannot force this process. Indeed, as Rogers warns, to force meaning on it is to declare war on yourself.

When people ask me how I came to know more about myself, I answer by saying, "by living." I am not trying to be cute or to oversimplify the sometimes painful process of embracing the shadows that have accumulated over the years in all of our lives, and often present themselves in the form of unfinished business that demands our attention. Nonetheless, I have discovered that the more I trust the natural processes of life, including those found in my own experiences, and learn from them, the more I move toward the person I am becoming. Listening to my own experiences, I discovered a little boy who was too sensitive for his own good, but whose sensitivity to the needs of others and the value of human relationships was his special gift to the world. Listening to my own experiences, I discovered places where I had been wounded, the times I felt disconfirmed because I was too soft or sensitive. I remembered how much it hurt and I used my pain to connect to others who might have been wounded in the same place.

In the process of learning to trust my experiences, I also learned to love myself for who I was and to quit trying to be what I wasn't. All my life I had believed that I needed to be "tougher"—more of a real man. Through listening to my experiences, trusting them to tell me things about myself, and accepting myself for who I was becoming, I learned that being a sensitive person is a wonderful person to be. I have applied this lesson to my thoughts about leadership styles and learned that it is best to be who you are in that role as well. Applying this lesson to my role in the organization, I have come to know that the world needs sensitive leaders. Listening to my experiences and learning to trust them to tell me valuable truths about myself, I have also discovered a pattern to my life, what those in the field of psychology call a *life theme* (Csikszentmihalyi, 1993; Rogers, 1961). The pattern in my life is connected by the theme of human relationships and expresses itself in the concept of a place to shine.

If I were to give any more advice related to getting to know and love yourself, it would be to reflect on those times in your life when you were the happiest, the times when you were so lost in enjoying what you were doing that time passed without you knowing it and you were absorbed in the moment to the extent that you even forgot yourself. Don't be too concerned about specifics. Rather, use all of your senses. Look for feelings, patterns, and interaction with others, things that transcend the particulars of one specific situation. For example, in reflecting on the times in my life when I was lost in what I was doing I have noted that it usually involved relating to others, philosophizing verbally and in writing, defending the underdog, and giving sermons—all things that I love to do and can be expressed in many different situations. As a result, I look for ways to shine by interacting with others, writing, and speaking even when I feel lost in the shadows at work.

When I let my experiences speak to me, they not only told me valuable things about myself, but they also pointed me to times when I had been wounded. I discovered that most of the wounds in my life were inflicted in a vulnerable spot, the spot where I am prone to feel less than adequate as a male because of my sensitivity to others and my fear of open conflict. I have learned from my wounds to be sensitive toward others who might have been wounded in a similar spot. I now go around helping myself and others learn how to be more open to the natural conflict in human relationships, not to shy away from it, but rather to learn from it and grow because of having lived through it.

Many people have been writing books lately about getting to know yourself. As a result, we are blessed with a plethora of models to help us in our search. But my advice would be to avoid getting hung up on models or being hard on yourself because you still can't quite figure out who you are or where your place to shine might be. Part of the answer could be right behind your nose, in your memory bank, the "full graineries of the past" as Viktor Frankl called them. If you listen to your experiences you will discover wonderful secrets about yourself. But most importantly, you will discover that you are far from finished. And you will be okay with that knowledge, even if it means you must trust the forces of life to take you toward your place to shine without knowing for certain where it will be. You will begin to appreciate your own potential and find comfort in the process of becoming.

STEP #2: LET GO

Having acknowledged many discoveries about myself in step one, including some issues in my life that I did not particularly want to deal with, the second bold step I had to take in my journey out from the shadows was to let go. This phrase had several meanings for me. On one level, letting go had to do with letting go of my need to control things and people. In fact, in an earlier version of this book I called this step "let 'my people' go" to make the point that as leaders we often think of the people who choose to follow our lead as "our people." I pointed out that letting my people go was something God and Moses negotiated with the Egyptians long ago. We do not own anyone—or motivate anyone for that matter. As leaders, the most we can do is inspire people to connect to their own place to shine and nurture the kind of environment where people are given the opportunity to make the right connections to others and shine in their work.

On another level I discovered that letting go had to do with the unfinished business in my life. I was spending my time absorbed in shoulds, oughts, and regrets. I discovered that part of the shadow side of my gift of sensitivity toward others was my need to please them. I was doing what I thought others wanted me to do and building up resentment toward them in the process. Learning that I had choices and letting go of my need to please everyone freed me to please both myself and others in ways that were more rewarding than before. In the process I also learned to let go of regrets over past decisions, to make my peace with an unfinished script in my head. I came to acknowledge that my decision to leave my studies toward the ministry to pursue a career in business, which I had thought was done only out of necessity, could be turned into a way to shine, perhaps even brighter than I would have had I become a preacher. As one who had lived in the shadows of the organization, I could reach an audience I never would have touched from the pulpit of a church.

Some of the stuff I had to let go of was paradoxical in nature. Let me explain. I grew up in a large family. Although we always had enough, we were still considered poor, at least by our own definition. Once one takes on the identity of being poor, rich people become the "other people." And the other people always have more faults than we do. To poor people, rich people are compromisers. They had to be in order to get rich. Otherwise how does one explain to oneself why one is not rich like them? It feels better to think that it was one's high morals that kept one from becoming well-off. This kind of thinking permeated my community and my family. Therefore, when I grew up and started making money, more money than my family ever saw and enough to be "well-off," I was faced with a real dilemma. On one hand I felt good about succeeding; on the other I felt guilty for having done so. "After all," I thought, "there must be something wrong with me. I must have compromised like all rich people do."

Psychologists remind us that it is natural to want more. Sometimes when we are not allowed to express this openly, we want what we can't have even more. As a child I wanted all the things that some of my friends had or that were displayed on the TV set every evening. At the same time, I felt guilty for wanting them. Ironically, to overcome this dilemma I had to let go of wanting to not succeed in order to let go of having to succeed. In other words, I had to tell myself that it was okay and indeed natural to want to succeed. Once I made peace with my natural human drive to want more, the need to succeed no longer possessed me. I had nothing to prove and I could shine without needing to succeed by the standards of the culture I live in. I could even redefine success on new, healthier terms.

Letting go means embracing the shadows of our past, learning to forgive ourselves and to love ourselves for who we are, human frailties and all. As hard as it is to do this, there is something magical about it. Letting go frees us to give to ourselves and others in ways that we never were able to before because our energy is no longer absorbed by regrets, shoulds, and oughts. We are free to shine.

STEP #3: GET TO KNOW OTHERS

Step three is closely connected to the first two steps. I learned more about myself from others than from myself. And I learned to let go of the need to control things and people as well as the regrets, shoulds, and oughts in my life by connecting to others. Once I learned to let go, I also learned that I was free to connect to others in more meaningful ways.

A central message of this book is that we get to know ourselves, including where we shine, by getting to know others. Thus, I have frequently quoted the words of Martin Buber, who reminded us that the self is an evolving or becoming concept that grows stronger and richer through interaction. As I have said so many times, shining is really about connecting, to ourselves, our work, each other, and purposes beyond the immediate. The self is confirmed and blossoms in the "inbetweenness" of our relationships to each other.

Carl Rogers, the therapist who wrote about the power of unconditional acceptance, suggested that the best way to help people shine was to accept them and believe in the positive forces at work in them. In step two I learned that this advice also applies to accepting oneself. But I think Rogers discovered something more than this. Like Buber, he had discovered the power of the "inbetweenness," the connections between people.

Getting to know others is a hard thing for leaders to do. We have been socialized to distance ourselves from our people. We dare not get intimate with them lest we expose ourselves to caring and the commitments of close relationships and thus lose our power over them. Contrary to this way of thinking, I have discovered that daring to get to know people does not take away my power, only my control over them. Getting to know people generates power. And losing control over them frees them to shine in ways that we never imagined.

STEP #4: CONNECT TO A PURPOSE

The fourth step that I had to take in order to emerge from the shadows at work was to connect to a purpose. Again, I discovered that step four was connected to the first three. While getting to know myself, letting go, and getting to know others, I was being found by a purpose.

Frederick Buechner discovered in his own life that purpose in work had to do with two dimensions. First, the purpose had to be personal. In other words, it needed to connect to one's gifts and experiences at a deep level. Second, the purpose needed to connect to a real need in the world. Buechner married this insight with the wonderful phrase "the place where your deep gladness and the world's deep hunger meet" (Buechner, 1973). Matthew Fox who more recently wrote about the need to reinvent work, including the need for purpose, said: "Often our work comes from a deep place of solitude. Perhaps if it comes from anywhere else it is not truly work but merely 'being worked' or having a job" (Fox, 1994). Both of these writers reaffirm the need for purpose in our work. Without it, we will not shine.

Mihaly Csikszentmihalyi, whom I have also quoted frequently, suggested that what we call "meaning" in Western societies has three dimensions. In one sense it points to an end, a purpose that is linked to an ultimate goal, a causal order to things such as *The meaning of life is to achieve self-awareness*. The second part has to do with intent or resolve, as implied in the statement *I mean to do well*. The third part involves the overall ordering of information or events, as in *Red sky in the evening means good weather in the morning* (Csikszentmihalyi, 1990). Csikszentmihalyi defined these three parts of meaning as *purpose, resolve,* and *harmony* and reminded us that the real meaning of life emerges from living it. In other words, life takes on meaning as we live it and put meaning into it through discovering *purpose* in our work, having the *resolve* to do something about it, and creating *harmony* by connecting it to a life theme and the universal theme of life itself.

A purpose to our work gives it a richness that merely holding a job or developing a career will never provide. It is a source of energy needed to help us shine. Ironically, we discover purpose when we connect to our work and each other. Or perhaps a sense of purpose and meaning finds us when we are doing what we love with people we love.

STEP #5: BECOME A MATCH-MAKER

Step five is one that is especially important for leaders. It is about matching people to their place to shine.

I have been told over the years that leadership is about recruiting the "right" people and then rewarding them with incentives. One manager I know talked about hiring ".300 hitters." My experience tells me different. I discovered that the most powerful groups to be around were those who consisted of people who had been passed over by the system. After all the noise about motivating and empowering people had died down in my ears, I learned that the best way to help people shine was to help them match their special gifts and experiences to a purpose in their work and to connect to each other. If I was able to help that process along, people would out-shine my greatest expectations. I learned that there is no greater feeling as a leader than to watch people exceed even their own expectations. With the division that cared, I had the privilege of watching a group of people out-shine their own expectations and experienced the awesome joy of being part of it. The only thing left to do was get out of the way.

I have come to believe that as leaders our primary role is to bring light into the system so that people can shine in their own special way in spite of the shadows in the system. A metaphor comes to mind when I dwell on this truth. I like to think of people as diamonds, each with their own special gifts that are like facets. Like diamonds, when the light hits the facets just right, people shine. Great leaders are like the jeweler who has mastered the art of bringing light to shine on the diamonds at angles that bring out the true beauty of each gem.

STEP #6: DARE TO CARE

Earlier I made the statement that all great leaders had one thing in common: followers. I lied. They have one other common quality. They care and it shows.

Commenting on the qualities of leaders in the miracle of South Africa in a recent presentation that I attended, Kobus Neethling referred to a passion that showed in words and actions. He accented the point that these leaders never gave up on their vision. Even in their moments of despair, they held on to their passion. Moreover, they blended their passion with compassion for people that showed in a willingness to forgive and to accept others unconditionally.

Those who have studied leadership in American corporations have noted the same qualities in great leaders. James Kouzes and Barry Posner cited credibility as a key quality of leadership. Their research showed that leaders must establish credibility in the eyes of those who chose to follow. Leaders who showed that they really cared for the people and for the task, even when the going got rough, were considered credible (Kouzes and Posner, 1987). And actions spoke much louder than words. Daring to care is a prerequisite to emerging from the shadows at work. Furthermore, it is a quality found in leaders and followers who are busy building places to shine.

STEP #7: SIMPLIFY, SIMPLIFY, SIMPLIFY!

The final step that I had to take in order to shine was to make things a whole lot simpler than I had. This truth applied to my personal life as well as my role as a leader.

In *Walden,* Henry David Thoreau reminded his readers that
the road to happiness was in a different direction than they had
been led to believe by the culture they lived in; it led away from
the complicated world of things and needing to possess them and
toward a simpler life connected to nature. "Our life is frittered
away by detail," he wrote. "An honest man has hardly need to
count more than his ten fingers, or in extreme cases he may add
his ten toes, and lump the rest. Simplicity, simplicity, simplicity!"
(Thoreau, 1854; 1981 ed.). His words have been echoed over the
years by others who have reflected on the "busyness" of our lives.
T. S. Eliot wrote:

> Where is the Life we have lost in living?
> Where is the knowledge we have lost in information?
> The cycles of Heaven in twenty centuries
> Bring us farther from God and nearer to the Dust.

Perhaps these philosophers of life have gone too far in the
direction of reflection and forgotten to balance it with the need to
actively engage in life and to grow through interacting with others, but they make a point nonetheless. Our world has become far
too complicated. And it is getting worse by the minute. Spurred
on by the need to restore our competitive position in the world,
we are working each other to death. The shadows of our "busyness" are getting in the way of our efforts to shine by connecting
to our work, each other, and purposes that transcend the immediate. It takes time to connect and to build healthier relationships.

My advice to you is to slow down and to connect. If you are
in the role of a leader, this advice extends to the need to simplify
our structures in ways that help people connect to their work, the
people they work with, and the customers they seek to delight. In
Chapter 16 I used the metaphor of cells to describe one way for
us to engage each other in the process of building places to shine.
It is a simple model, intended to show how we can simplify our
work environment so that people can connect to their work and
each other again and experience the joy and power of play in their

work. It is not the only model for simplifying our structures at work. There are many models to choose from. Many of these options are discussed in Chapter 13. However, my intent is not to offer the best design for your particular business. Rather, it is to remind us all about the human side of structures and to point out that we shine our brightest when our structures are simple enough for us to connect our special gifts to purposes and to share them with others. If our structures stay so complicated that we cannot see what is going on or understand the mission and vision of our organization and feel it in our hearts, we will not shine in our work. I hope that this is a lesson we have learned from living in the shadows of the industrial era and one that we will take with us into the next millennium.

In this chapter, I have shared seven bold steps that helped me get started on my own journey to a place to shine. I hope that they will prove to be of help to you on your own journey. Perhaps the most valuable advice I can offer is that you begin to share your desire for meaning and purpose in your work, including your need to shine, with others—because the power of connecting is still the most powerful force I can think of.

_____ AN EPILOGUE:

The Beginning

A Place to Shine is not a perfect place to which we travel or a
utopia that we create. Rather, it is a place for caring and
connecting along the way.

> . . . DANIEL S. HANSON

Now that I have finished this book I can't help but wonder:
was it worth it? Will the insights that I shared make a difference
in the lives of people? The answer that comes back to me is: I don't
know. But as I speculated in the Introduction, perhaps all any
writer can do is to offer up his or her thoughts and hope that the
reader continues the dialogue. Faced with this same dilemma,
Pulitzer Prize–winning author Ernest Becker wrote: "The most
that any of us can seem to do is to fashion something—an object
or ourselves—and drop it into the confusion, make an offering of
it, so to speak, to the life force" (Becker, 1973). In this spirit, I offer
my final thoughts—not as the end of a book, but rather as the beginning of an ongoing dialogue.

In the Introduction I listed four objectives:

1. To restore faith in the human spirit and the creative drive in
each of us to shine in our work

2. To expose the shadows in the organization that keep people from shining in their work
3. To offer a language and some tools to stimulate the ongoing dialogue and encourage groups of people to build their own places to shine
4. To show by word and example that accepting each other with unconditional regard and confirming the potential in each other through healthy interaction produces an energy force that brings out the light within, between, and around us and helps us shine even in the shadows

I will never feel certain that I accomplished these objectives. I can only hope that I started something that will take on a life of its own and move in a positive direction that will continue long after this book is out of print. Throughout the process of writing this book I searched for a metaphor that would bring these ideas to life. I tried to find a metaphor to describe the process of bringing light into our work so that everyone can shine. I played with the idea of "candles in the night." I looked at cells of people as the cells of a battery that, when connected, form a circuit that generates electricity and light. I considered beams of light that spread out their rays to touch other beams of light. All these were wonderful metaphors with real potential for expanding the messages that I was trying to get across. But I finally landed on a metaphor that seems to work the best for me even though it does not immediately evoke images of light. I will share it in the hope that it will offer a proper beginning for the end of this book.

I look at this book as a packet of seeds that I have thrown out to the public. Whether or not these seeds will grow into anything of value depends on the care and nurturing they receive from others— and the light that is brought to shine on them. For example, if these seeds are not cultivated by the ongoing dialogue of others who care about the same issues, weeds will grow up and block out the light, thus creating more shadows to keep people from shining in their work. If these seeds are not watered by the rich rain of other truths and fertilized by new ideas, they will wither and die. If these seeds that I have planted do not receive the light of confirmation that can only come from people accepting each other and caring for each other, they will not grow and reach their potential. Thus, this book is only as good as the light it brings out in others who care.

I believe that the light is out there. I believe that these seeds will blend with the seeds cast by you and others to form a garden of rich ideas. I believe that these ideas will take root and blossom into words and deeds that will transform our places of work into places to shine. What I have offered here is only the beginning.

QUESTIONS FOR FURTHER DIALOGUE

Work in a New Light
What changes have you seen in the workplace as it relates to theories about people and work, structures, or scripts? Are they healthy changes?

What are the terms of the new social contract at work? What commitments or attachments are implied?

Theories Based on the Human Spirit
If you were rewriting the theories about people, work, and organizations, what would they be? What are the underlying assumptions you would use? What metaphors would describe people? Work? Organizations?

Structures Around People and Purposes
How would you structure the organization to make room for people to shine in their work? What would hold the structure together?

What are the risks associated with new structures? How would you minimize these risks?

Caring, Connecting, and Confirming Scripts
How would you approach the delicate issue of "put-downs" and unhealthy scripts using the approach of systems thinking, skill development, building trust through intimacy, or an

approach of your own? What are the risks associated with intimacy in the work place? How should they be dealt with?

Do you know people who are interpersonally competent? How do they present themselves or what do they do that seems to work?

Describe a conflict situation that was handled poorly. Then describe one that was handled well. What was it about each situation that resulted in learning?

The Power of Connecting
What phase of the transformation process described in Chapter 16 is your organization experiencing? Describe the clouds that you are dealing with.

Have you ever experienced the power of connecting to a task and a group of people who care? Describe the circumstances.

Leadership in a New Light
So much has been written about leadership. What does leadership mean to you? How would it unfold and what would leaders be like in a place to shine?

Do you know someone whom you consider a real leader? Describe him or her.

Seven Bold Steps
What are some of the steps that you have taken on your journey to a place to shine? How do they compare to the steps I described in Chapter 18?

Has this book changed your thinking about people, work, or organizations? If so, in what way?

References

Argyris, Chris. *Knowledge for Action: A Guide for Overcoming Barriers to Organizational Change.* San Francisco: Jossey-Bass, 1993.

Autry, James. *Love and Profit: The Art of Caring Leadership.* New York: William Morrow, 1991.

Becker, Ernest. *The Denial of Death.* New York: The Free Press, 1973.

———. *Escape From Evil.* New York: The Free Press, 1975.

Bellah, Robert N., Richard Madsen, William M. Sullivan, Ann Swidler, and Steven M. Tipton. *Habits of the Heart.* New York: Harper & Row, 1985.

———. *The Good Society.* New York: Vintage, 1992.

Bennis, Warren. *On Becoming a Leader.* Reading, Mass.: Addison-Wesley, 1989.

Bender, Sue. *Plain and Simple.* New York: Harper Collins, 1989.

Bettelheim, Bruno. *The Informed Heart.* New York: Macmillan, 1960.

Bormann, Ernest. *Small Group Communication: Theory and Practice.* 3rd ed. New York: Harper & Row, 1990.

Borysenko, Joan. *Fire in the Soul.* New York: Warner, 1993.

Brey, Douglas, and Ann Howard. *Managerial Lives in Transition: Advancing Age and Changing Times.* New York: Guilford Press, 1988.

Buechner, Frederick. *Wishful Thinking.* New York: Harper & Row, 1973.

———. *The Sacred Journey.* New York: Harper Collins, 1982.

———. *Telling Secrets.* San Francisco: Harper Collins, 1991.

Cohen, Michael D., James C. March, and Johan P. Olsen. "A Garbage Can Model of Organizational Choice." *Administrative Science Quarterly* 17, no. 1 (March 1972): 1–25.

Csikszentmihalyi, Mihaly. *Flow: The Psychology of Optimal Experience.* New York: Harper & Row, 1990.

———. *The Evolving Self.* New York: Harper Collins, 1993.

Foster, W. "Toward a Critical Practice of Leadership," in J. Smyth, Ed. *Critical Perspectives on Educational Leadership.* New York: Palmer Press, 1992: 39–62.

Fox, Matthew. *A New Vision of Livelihood for Our Time.* San Francisco: Harper Collins, 1994.

Frankl, Viktor. *Man's Search for Meaning.* Boston: Beacon, 1984.

Friedman, Maurice, ed. Martin Buber: *The Knowledge of Man.* New York: Harper & Row, 1965.

Fromm, Erich. *The Heart of Man.* New York: Harper & Row, 1964.

Frost, Gerhard. *Bless My Growing.* Minneapolis: Augsburg, 1974.

Galbraith, Jay R. *Designing Organizations.* San Francisco: Jossey-Bass, 1995.

Gardner, Howard. *Frames of Mind.* New York: Basic Books, 1985.

Gergen, K., and M. Gergen, eds. *Historical Social Psychology.* Hillsdale, N.J.: Erlbaum, 1984.

Glasser, William. *Control Theory.* New York: Harper & Row, 1984.

Goffman, Erving. *The Presentation of Self in Everyday Life.* New York: Doubleday, 1959.

———. *Asylums.* New York: Doubleday, 1961.

Greenleaf, Robert K. *Servant Leadership.* New York: Paulist Press, 1977.

Hagberg, Janet. *Real Power.* Rev. ed. Salem, Wis.: Sheffield, 1994.

Hall, Edward. *Beyond Culture.* New York: Doubleday, 1976.

Handy, Charles. *The Age of Unreason.* Boston: Harvard Business School Press, 1990.

———. *The Age of Paradox.* Boston: The Harvard Business School Press, 1994.

Helgeson, Sally. *The Web of Inclusion.* New York: Doubleday, 1995.

Hueber, G. "Baby Boomer's Look to Lives Outside Work for Fulfillment." *Minneapolis Star & Tribune.* April 7, 1991.

Kaufmann, Walter, ed. *The Portable Nietzsche.* New York: Penguin, 1976.

Kohn, Alfie. *Punished by Rewards: The Trouble with GOLD STARS, IN-CENTIVE PLAN$, A's, PRAISE and Other Bribes.* Boston: Houghton Mifflin, 1993.

Konner, Melvin. *The Tangled Wing.* New York: Harper & Row, 1987.

Kouzes, James M., and Barry Z. Posner. *The Leadership Challenge.* San Francisco: Jossey-Bass, 1987.

———. *Credibility.* San Francisco: Jossey-Bass, 1993.

Kuhn, Manfred H. "The Reference Group Reconsidered," *Sociological Quarterly* 5, Winter, 1964b.

LaBier, Douglas. *Modern Madness: The Emotional Fallout of Success.* Reading, Mass.: Addison-Wesley, 1986.

Lasch, Christopher. *The Minimal Self.* New York: W. W. Norton, 1984.

Lee, Dorothy. *Freedom and Culture.* Prospect Heights, Ill.: Waveland Press, 1987.

Lipnack, Jessica, and Jeffrey Stamps. *The TeamNet Factor.* Essex Junction, Vt.: Oliver Wight Publications, 1993.

Lulic, Margaret. *Who We Could Be at Work.* rev. ed. Newton, Mass.: Butterworth-Heinemann, 1996.

Maccoby, Michael. *The Leader.* New York: Ballantine Books, 1983.

———. *Why Work: Leading the New Generation.* New York: Simon and Schuster, 1988.

Mead, George H. *Mind, Self and Society.* Chicago: The University Press, 1967.

Mumford, Lewis. *Technics and Civilization.* New York: Harcourt, 1963.

O'Day, Rory. "Intimidation Rituals: Reactions to Reform." *The Journal of Applied Behavioral Science* 10, no. 3 (1974): 373–386.

Olmsted, Michael S., and Paul A. Hare. *The Small Group.* New York: Random House, 1978.

Peck, M. Scott. *The Different Drum: Community Making and Peace.* New York: Simon & Schuster, 1987.

———. *A World Waiting to be Born.* New York: Bantam, 1993.

Perrow, Charles. *Complex Organizations: A Critical Essay.* 3rd ed. New York: Random House, 1986.

Reich, Robert. *The Work of Nations.* New York: Alfred A. Knopf, 1991.

Rogers, Carl R. *On Becoming A Person.* Boston: Houghton Mifflin, 1961.

Savage, Charles. *5th Generation Management.* rev. ed. Newton, Mass.: Butterworth- Heinemann, 1996.

Schaef, Anne Wilson. *Women's Reality.* New York: Harper Collins, 1991.

Schaef, Anne Wilson, and Dianne Fassel. *The Addictive Organization.* New York: Harper & Row, 1988.

Schor, Juliet. *The Overworked American: The Unexpected Decline of Leisure.* New York: Harper Collins, 1991.

Schumacher, E. F. *Small Is Beautiful: Economics as if People Mattered.* New York: Harper & Row, 1975.

Senge, Peter. *The Fifth Discipline.* New York: Doubleday, 1994.

Sinetar, Marsha. *Developing a 21st Century Mind*. New York: Ballantine, 1991.

Stogdill, R. M. *Handbook of Leadership*. New York: The Free Press, 1974.

Thoreau, Henry David. *Walden*. Norwalk, Conn.: The Easton Press, 1981.

Wheatley, Margaret J. *Leadership and the New Science*. San Francisco: Berrett-Koehler, 1994.

Wing, R. *The Tao of Power*. New York: Doubleday, 1986.

Wink, Walter. *Engaging the Powers*. Minneapolis: Fortress Press, 1992.

Index